STUDY GROUP PAPERS

The U.S.-Japan Security Alliance in the 21st Century

Prospects for Incremental Change

Michael J. Green
and
Mike M. Mochizuki

Background papers from the
Study Group on the U.S.-Japan Security Alliance

Bruce Stokes, Project Director
Harold Brown and Richard Armitage, Co-Chairs

BLH 0567- 7/1

e Council on Foreign Relations, Inc., a nonprofit, nonpartisan national memship organization founded in 1921, is dedicated to promoting understanding
nternational affairs through the free and civil exchange of ideas. The Counmembers are dedicated to the belief that America's peace and prosperity are
1ly linked to that of the world. From this flows the mission of the Council:
foster America's understanding of its fellow members of the international
1munity, near and far, their peoples, cultures, histories, hopes, quarrels and ambis; and thus to serve, protect, and advance America's own global interests through
ly and debate, private and public.

E COUNCIL TAKES NO INSTITUTIONAL POSITION
POLICY ISSUES AND HAS NO AFFILIATION WITH THE
. GOVERNMENT. ALL STATEMENTS OF FACT AND
__.PRESSIONS OF OPINION CONTAINED IN ALL ITS
PUBLICATIONS ARE THE SOLE RESPONSIBILITY OF THE
AUTHOR OR AUTHORS.

*Council on Foreign Relations Books are distributed by Brookings Institution Press
(1-800-275-1447). For further information on Council publications, please write
the Council on Foreign Relations, 58 East 68th Street, New York, NY 10021, or
call the Public Affairs Office at (212) 434-9400.*

Copyright © 1998 by the Council on Foreign Relations®, Inc.
All Rights Reserved.
Printed in the United States of America.

This report may not be reproduced, in whole or in part, in any form (beyond that
copying permitted by Sections 107 and 108 of the U.S. Copyright Law and
excerpts by reviewers for the public press), without written permission from the
publishers. For information, write Publications Office, Council on Foreign Relations, 58 East 68th Street, New York, NY 10021.

CONTENTS

FOREWORD

The future of the U.S.-Japan alliance is in doubt. Events such as the 1995 rape incident in Okinawa and massive public demonstrations in Japan against the U.S. troop presence have forced Washington and Tokyo to acknowledge facts: the relationship they forged during the Cold War must change with changing times. The Council on Foreign Relations accordingly formed a Study Group, chaired by Harold Brown of CSIS and Richard Armitage of Armitage Associates, to reexamine assumptions and explore the factors affecting the evolution of this crucial alliance.

A Report by the Study Group Project Director, James Shinn, has been published in English and Japanese. The two essays in this volume contributed to the deliberations of the Study Group by assessing underlying forces.

These essays demonstrate how tricky the business of reforming the alliance will be. To begin with, both the United States and Japan have vested interests in keeping things exactly as they are now. So do other countries in the region, especially China and South Korea. Michael Green outlines a number of scenarios that could challenge the alliance's tradition of slow evolution—including a protracted war in Korea or confrontation with China—but warns that planning for those scenarios could undermine rather than strengthen the alliance.

Furthermore, inside Japan, the end of the Cold War and the Liberal Democratic Party's hegemony has eroded the generally pro-American consensus that was the hallmark of Japan's postwar foreign policy. Indeed, younger policymakers whose experience is not shaped by the lessons of the Second World War and the Cold War have begun to question the merits of the pro-American consensus. Mike Mochizuki argues that, although there is currently broad Japanese agreement on maintaining security ties with the United States, competing opinion clusters already vie for influence in shaping Japan's post–Cold War identity as either a "civilian" or a "normal" power.

The governments of the United States and Japan would be wrong to cling to the status quo rather than face these challenges. The current alliance may be adequate to meet the requirements of stability and security in Northeast Asia today, but the dangers of tomorrow could severely test and even threaten the existence of an alliance that does not evolve. Radical change is neither necessary nor desirable. Rather, Washington and Tokyo should promote a slow and steady evolution that reflects changing regional and domestic conditions. Their September 1997 revision of the defense guidelines—which elucidated and moderately strengthened Japan's role within the alliance—showed an awareness of the need for periodic adaptation. In this fashion, the alliance must remain dynamic, if only through incremental change, to continue underpinning the stability of Asia.

Gary C. Hufbauer
Director of Studies
Council on Foreign Relations
November 1997

Interests, Asymmetries, and Strategic Choices

Michael J. Green

INTRODUCTION

STRUCTURAL REALISTS HAVE long doubted that the U.S.-Japan alliance can survive into the next century, given the asymmetries between the two countries.[1] The 1960 Treaty of Mutual Security and Cooperation commits the United States to defend Japan (Article V), while Japan's contribution to U.S. and regional security is not spelled out beyond its pledge to provide facilities to U.S. forces "for the purpose of contributing to the security of Japan and the maintenance of international peace and security in the Far East" (Article VI). This unequal arrangement has survived not only the growth of Japan's economy to rival that of the United States, but also the end of the Cold War and the decline of the Soviet threat in the Far East.

Are the structural realists wrong? Not necessarily. The alliance has thrived despite its asymmetries because it has served the fundamental interests of both parties throughout the Cold War and in the current strategic environment. In fact, the asymmetries themselves have arguably suited both parties. However, if the alliance's international context were to change—whether through a military crisis in the region, the emergence of a hegemonic rival to the United States, or the mitigation of strategic rivalry through regional economic integration—then the asymmetries could make the alliance

---

1. Structural realists believe that relative power determines all outcomes in the international system. Therefore, given its growing economic power relative to the United States, Japan is unlikely to accept military dependency indefinitely and will eventually increase its independent military capabilities. The best-known exponent of this thesis is Henry Kissinger.

[1]

unsustainable in its present form. Internal political factors in the United States and Japan, such as ascendant nationalism or isolationism, could further complicate matters.

To date, the alliance has successfully evolved in response to shifts in the domestic and international environments. The quid pro quo achieved at the April 1996 security summit (following the "Nye Initiative") is a recent example of an incremental "redefinition" of the security relationship: Japan agreed to consider a supporting role in a regional contingency (through the Guidelines Review), [MCAS] and the United States agreed to return facilities on Okinawa (Futenma Marine Corps Air Station).[2] Previous examples of redefinition of the alliance include the 1960 treaty revision, the 1969 Sato-Nixon Communiqué, the 1978 Guidelines for Defense Cooperation, and the evolution of the approach to roles and missions during the 1980s.[3]

The United States and Japan, therefore, have demonstrated a modest ability to adjust the alliance to meet changing strategic and domestic political contexts. Structural realists would argue, however, that

---

2. The "Nye Initiative," also known as the "Japan Security Dialogue," was an intensive bilateral review of the U.S.-Japan alliance aimed at coordinating long-term security planning (such as the U.S. East Asian Strategic Report and Japan's National Defense Program Outline). The effort started in fall 1995 and culminated in the April 1996 Security Declaration.

3. The 1960 revision of the Security Treaty withdrew U.S. responsibility for domestic stability in Japan and brought "mutuality" to the security relationship. The 1969 Sato-Nixon Communiqué announced the return of Okinawa to Japanese territory and made the first explicit reference to Japanese interests in regional security (specifically the security of Taiwan and Korea). This pattern was similar in many ways to the April 1996 Joint Security Declaration, which announced the U.S. decision to return Futenma air base and the decision to revise the 1978 Guidelines for Defense Cooperation to focus on "situations in the area around Japan." The 1978 guidelines were significant because they represented the first effort to authorize defense planning between U.S. and Japanese forces. The focus of the guidelines was the defense of Japan against direct attack, however, and there was little in the document to reflect the 1969 Sato-Nixon Communiqué's focus on regional security. Explicit authority for a regional dimension to defense planning would have to wait two more decades. In the interim, however, the 1978 guidelines did provide a framework for bilateral defense cooperation that enhanced the legitimacy of Japan's Self-Defense Forces and strengthened military-to-military ties between the two countries. This precedent opened the way for the "Roles and Missions" approach of the Reagan administration, which established the "sword" and "spear" division of labor between U.S. and Japanese forces and locked the "defense of Japan" into larger U.S. regional strategies for containing the Soviet Union.

more radical changes will be necessary if the alliance is to endure. Contemplation of more ambitious changes to the alliance structure, however, requires an appreciation of the reasons for the current asymmetries and the relative costs and benefits of attempting to change them.

The aim of this essay is to establish a framework for discussion of the strategic choices available to the United States and Japan. In pursuit of that goal, the paper:

• Catalogues U.S. and Japanese interests that underpin the alliance;

• Delineates the alliance's asymmetries and assesses the possible consequences of attempting to rectify them in the current strategic and political environment;

• Assesses the consequences of not addressing those asymmetries in a changed strategic environment (on the basis of four alternative scenarios for the future).

While the present structure of the U.S.-Japan alliance may be appropriate in the current environment, it may not suffice to meet future challenges. Yet pushing for the alliance of tomorrow could undermine the objectives of the alliance of today. This essay, with its systematic approach, provides a backdrop for the subsequent examination of the alliance from the Japanese perspective.

THE ALLIANCE AND NATIONAL INTERESTS

The present asymmetries in the alliance make sense because they serve fundamental interests of each country.

The United States

Political and economic influence
Through its bilateral alliances with Japan and South Korea, the United States uses its military presence to influence political and economic developments in the region (though its leverage is often squandered and may be declining).

Regional stability
The U.S.-Japan alliance helps to prevent the emergence of destabilizing military rivalries between Japan, South Korea, and China.

Containment of rival hegemons
Throughout the Cold War, the U.S.-Japan alliance prevented the expansion of Soviet power in the region (and in the future it may be used for the same purposes against an increasingly powerful China).

Economic access
The alliance contributes to the stability that is the basis for East Asia's dynamic economic growth, from which the United States derives direct economic benefit (including $400 billion in annual trans-Pacific trade and 3 million American jobs linked to that trade and investment).

Burden-sharing
Paying over $4 billion annually in host nation support, Japan underwrites a significant portion of the U.S. forward presence in the region (even if expectations for greater burden-sharing in areas such as technology have gone unfulfilled).

Deterrence/war-fighting capabilities
U.S. bases in Japan allow the United States to launch effective military operations in the region.

Global partnership
The alliance forms the basis for bilateral cooperation on global issues, including the United Nations, arms control, and Middle East peace.

Japan

Regional stability
The United States and Japan share an interest in preventing the emergence of military rivalry among the economic powers of Northeast Asia.

[4]

Michael J. Green

Domestic prosperity
In the postwar period, the U.S.-Japan alliance was essential to the consolidation of a stable conservative political force—the Liberal Democratic Party (LDP)—that made Japan's economic growth possible.

Containment of rival hegemons
Japanese leaders came to accept and support U.S. strategies of containment against the Soviet Union, and current uncertainty about China's future has reinforced Japanese interest in this aspect of the alliance.

Avoidance of conflict
Japan's alliance management has consistently aimed at avoiding actual participation (*makikomareru*) in U.S. conflicts, from Vietnam to the Persian Gulf, which could undermine Japan's domestic stability and regional role.

Mercantile freedom
The alliance undergirds the freedom of commercial activity in Asia (and—until the 1970s—insulated Japan from U.S. competition in its domestic market).

Global partnership
Japan's alliance with the United States has been a key factor in Tokyo's growing role in multilateral institutions such as the United Nations, the Asian Development Bank, and the Organization for Economic Cooperation and Development. In recent years, U.S. and Japanese interests have diverged somewhat in policy decisions at the World Bank and personnel decisions at the United Nations, but on the whole, Japan still derives significant benefit from partnership with the United States in regional and global multilateral institutions.

ALLIANCE ASYMMETRIES

How might the United States and Japan redress the present asymmetries with minimal effects on the above interests? Commentators tend to recommend restructuring the alliance in six areas:

• Reducing U.S. bases;[4]

• Expanding Japan's operational role;[5]

• Increasing Japan's political role;[6]

• Increasing technology reciprocity;[7]

• Expanding the role of multilateral security arrangements;[8]

• Using the security relationship as leverage to open Japanese markets.[9]

---

4. Reduction of all U.S. forces over the long term is advocated by Chalmers Johnson (with Barry Keehn) in "The Pentagon's Ossified Strategy," *Foreign Affairs*, (July/August 1995), and Jitsuro Terashima in "Shin Bei Nya Sogosenryaku o Mitomete," *Chuo Koron* (March 1996). The platform of Japan's new Democratic Party also calls for the eventual elimination of U.S. bases in Japan. Others, such as Mike Mochizuki and Satoshi Morimoto, advocate a significant reduction in the Marine Corps presence on Okinawa. See Mike M. Mochizuki and Michael O'Hanlon, "The Marines Should Come Home: Adapting the U.S.-Japan Alliance to a New Security Era," *Brookings Review* (Spring 1996), pp. 10–13.

5. Expanding Japan's operational role to include more combatant missions in regional contingencies is advocated by former Ambassador Hisahiko Okazaki, among others.

6. Maintaining the current alliance framework while expanding Japan's "civilian" political role is advocated by many experts, including Ed Lincoln in *Japan's New Global Role* (Washington, DC: Brookings Institution, 1993) and Kenneth Damm, John Deutch, Joseph Nye, Jr., and David M. Rowe in "Coping with Japan: The U.S. Strategy for Managing Japan's Rise as a Global Power," *Washington Quarterly* (Spring 1993).

7. See "Maximizing U.S. Interests in Science and Technology Relations with Japan," Report of the Defense Task Force (National Research Council, 1995).

8. Multilateral security structures are embraced by the *Asahi Shimbun*, the Socialist Party, and other constituencies concerned that too much bilateral defense cooperation with the United States would jeopardize Japan's constitutional framework.

9. See Johnson and Keehn, "The Pentagon's Ossified Strategy." See also Clyde Prestowitz, *Trading Places: How America Allowed Japan to Take the Lead* (New York: Basic Books, 1988) for an argument that trade and security priorities should be reversed. For a more nuanced linkage of trade and security policies, see Henry Nau, *Trade and Security: U.S. Policies at Cross Purposes* (Washington, DC: American Enterprise Institute, 1995).

Michael J. Green

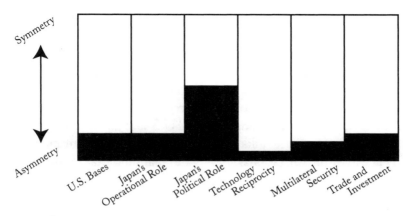

Figure 1. Current Asymmetries in the U.S.-Japan Alliance (Illustrative)

Each of these structural changes would address asymmetries in the alliance, while not eliminating them. Figure 1 illustrates the degree of structural change that each of these policy prescriptions might represent, with the vertical axis representing the level of symmetry.

Of course, specific asymmetries do not mean that the alliance is asymmetrical; in fact, attempting to correct them would risk undermining American and Japanese interests at both the macro and the micro levels. At the macro level, structural asymmetries serve the broad national interests of each side. At the micro level, key constituencies in each country also wish to maintain asymmetries. Several examples can be cited.

U.S. bases contribute to the defense of Japan and the stability of the region. Withdrawal of a significant part of the Third Marine Expeditionary Force (III MEF) from Okinawa, for example, would have operational consequences for U.S. capabilities and psychological consequences for regional stability. As an expeditionary force, III MEF also protects U.S.—and, implicitly, Japanese—interests as far away as the Gulf. Given U.S. defense budget constraints and the fact that Japanese host nation support covers 70 percent of the cost of stationing the marines, it is questionable whether III MEF could exist anywhere but Okinawa. The loss of Okinawan bases, in other words, could mean the loss of Marine Corps presence in Japan, with consequences for a whole range of U.S. and Japanese security interests.

Japan's operational role is still limited by Article IX of its constitution to the defense of Japan. The constitutional ban on the right to collective defense has come under scrutiny with the current review of the Defense Guidelines, which explicitly expand cooperation to cover regional contingencies that affect Japan's security. However, for reasons relating to overall U.S. and Japanese interests, both governments are unlikely to push the issue of constitutionality ahead of the operational studies and planning that result from the review.[10] Pushing the right to collective defense would provide clarity (in terms of what Japan could do) for joint planning, but it might also undermine the Japanese domestic political consensus that has allowed the unprecedented review to occur; it could fuel uncertainty and rivalry in relations with the Koreas and China as well. Consequently, the most the review can accomplish at this stage is to advance the process of mutual preparation for Japan's "rear-area" support role in the event of a regional conflict. This is a significant step forward from the 1978 Guidelines, which left the issue of Japan's role in a regional contingency deliberately vague, but the alliance will still lack the military and operational symmetry of NATO.

Japan's political role has expanded to complement other elements of the alliance relationship. Japan is playing a larger role in multilateral institutions such as Asia-Pacific Economic Cooperation and the United Nations, in arms control, in overseas development assistance, and in a variety of global issues captured under the U.S.-Japan Common Agenda. This global partnership is reaping diminishing returns, however, for two reasons related to the alliance structure. First, Japan's enthusiasm for a permanent U.N. Security Council seat has waned with the realization that Tokyo will be expected to pay more, take more diplomatic risks, and possibly play a larger military role in peacekeeping. Second, Japan does not fully

---

10. In the December 2, 1996, U.S.-Japan Defense Summit in Tokyo, U.S. Secretary of Defense William Perry and his Japanese counterparts reiterated their intention to proceed with the Guidelines Review "within the context of Japan's Constitutional Framework" (*Asahi Shimbun*, December 3, 1996). It is worth noting that an LDP Security "Project Team" issued a report the same week advocating recognition of the right to collective defense—a sign that steady, incremental change will continue. See *Sankei Shimbun*, November 30, 1996.

benefit from a global security partnership with the United States because Japan insists that the U.S.-Japan Security Treaty applies only to the "Far East." For example, Japanese support for the U.S. air strike on Iraq in September 1996 was political and implicitly operational (the Japanese press reported that U.S. bases in Japan were involved), but the Japanese government could only acknowledge its political support and consequently was relegated to a passive supporting role with limited influence on U.S. strategy.

Technological cooperation is still characterized by one-way flows of defense technology to Japan from the United States. While important precedents are being established for the reverse flow of technology through the Systems & Technology Forum and the F-2 project, reciprocity is still a long way off. The reasons for the continuing asymmetry are embedded in the interest group politics of each country. First, Japan's ban on arms exports (the Three Arms Export Principles) removes the incentive for Japanese defense companies to share technology, since there will not be a return on the investment at the development or production stages. Second, the Japanese companies that develop the most advanced dual-use technologies are not traditional defense contractors and are generally reluctant to work with the Pentagon. Third, U.S. defense contractors focus almost entirely on the Japanese defense market, and do not wish to unleash a new international competitor by advocating the end of the export ban. Finally, most U.S. program executive officers and defense labs see little advantage in disturbing and possibly tangling the complicated web of international cooperation, particularly with Japan.[11] The most important constituencies on each side are thus satisfied with the status quo, in spite of the resulting asymmetries.

Multilateral security was part of the focus of the April 1996 Security Declaration, a striking contrast to past joint summit statements on the alliance. Given the growing fluidity of power relations in East Asia, multilateral security dialogue could play an increas-

---

11. See Michael J. Green and Richard Samuels, "U.S.-Japan Defense Technology Cooperation: Ten Guidelines to Make It Work," MIT-Japan Program Working Paper (July 1994). Note that the Three Arms Export Principles were essentially amended in 1983 when Japan agreed to transfer militarily applicable technology to the United States through a joint committee.

ingly important role in regional stability. Nevertheless, the most developed forum at present–the ASEAN Regional Forum (ARF)–has addressed few substantive security issues beyond transparency. Meanwhile, a Northeast Asian security forum has been endorsed by many diplomats and scholars, but rejected by the two Koreas. Multilateral dialogue is no longer viewed as a threat to the bilateral alliance, but neither is it seen as a substitute.

Trade and investment are still out of balance between the United States and Japan. Japan's phenomenally low rate of foreign direct investment has not changed as a percentage of GNP in three decades; Japan continues to maintain many opaque public and private barriers to imports; and Japan persistently runs a large current account surplus with the rest of the world. But chronic imbalances have yet to seriously undermine American public support for the security relationship, possibly because the United States is presently "winning" the contest for economic growth.

Meanwhile, U.S. trade negotiators can expect diminishing returns as sectoral talks are replaced by firm-specific cases (e.g., within the insurance or film industries). While deregulation presents an opportunity, there are no powerful U.S. constituencies for Japanese deregulation per se. In fact, many are already "inside the moat" and thus quietly accept a regulated environment.

Trade and investment friction could poison the atmosphere of the alliance, though interdependence is probably too deeply rooted to allow a full-scale commercial war. At the same time, serious economic fatigue and limited U.S. resources have implications for America's ability to deploy troops abroad and thus to support the alliance.

The asymmetries in the alliance are thus awkward and potentially unsustainable, but continue to make sense because they serve critical U.S. and Japanese interests and are backed by powerful constituencies in each country. Dramatic steps to redistribute responsibilities within the alliance could lead to uncertain and potentially negative outcomes—an important consideration when East Asia is itself in an era of uncertainty.

The following matrix illustrates the potential consequences of structural change in the alliance in the current strategic environment. The horizontal axis lists the U.S. and Japanese interests described

INTERESTS

Policy Prescription	U.S.							JAPAN					
	Presence and Influence	Regional Stability	Containment	Economic Access	Burden-Sharing	Deterrence/Capabilities	Global Partnership	Regional Stability	Domestic Stability	Containment	Avoid Conflict	Mercantile Freedom	Global Partnership
Reduce U.S. Bases	-	-	-	-/?		-	-/?	-	+/?	-			-/?
Increase Japan's Operational Role	-	+/?		+	+	+/?		-	-	+/?	-	-/?	+/?
Expand Japan's Political Role						+		+/?		-/?	-/?		+/?
Technology Reciprocity		-/?		+/?	+/?	+/?		-/?	-				
Multilateralism	+/?	+/?				-		+/?	+/?				
Leverage Security for Trade & Investment	-	-		+/?	+/?	-/?		-	-			-	

Figure 2. Impact of Restructuring the Alliance in the Current Environment

earlier, and the vertical axis lists the policy prescriptions for correcting asymmetries in the alliance. The contents of the box (positive, negative, or uncertain) are based on the considerations listed in this section.

THREATS

The rigidities inherent in the status quo are understandable and largely appropriate, but will the alliance continue to serve American and Japanese interests in a changed context? The current review of the 1978 Defense Guidelines seeks to establish political and eventually legal authority for the Japanese government to support the United States in a regional contingency affecting Japan's security.

A rear-area Japanese role has now become acceptable domestically and in the region: it represents not an expansion of Japan's role but a clarification. During the Cold War, Japan's location between the Soviet Union and the rest of Asia allowed it to explain its role in U.S. strategy as pure self-defense based on Article V of the treaty. The demise of the Soviet threat has forced Japan to explain its supporting role in the event Japan is not the first target, and to clarify its role under Article VI. The Japanese rear-area role preserves the current asymmetries in the alliance and in the short term will probably keep the Japan Self-Defense Forces within an expanded definition of self-defense without crossing the line to collective defense (although this will be decided by Japan's Cabinet Legal Affairs Bureau in the wake of the Guidelines Review and the ensuing political debate).[12]

It is possible to speculate on any number of endogenous and exogenous changes that might threaten the current alliance structure, but four stand out: 1) a Korean contingency; 2) the emergence of a hostile Sino-U.S. relationship; 3) less sparkling U.S. economic performance; and 4) greater economic integration and confidence in the region.[13]

Korean Contingency

In the event of a North Korean attack on the South, the United States would probably seek at a minimum Japanese rear-area support. If the conflict were to spill offshore or involve missile or air attacks beyond the Peninsula, Japan might contribute to air and sea-lane defense. Prompt, robust, and well-planned Japanese support for U.S. forces would probably bring the U.S.-Japan alliance safely through a Korean conflict, provided that the termination of hostilities came quickly and the U.S.-ROK side was victorious.

---

12. Ultimately, this interpretation will depend on Japanese domestic politics and the judgment of the Cabinet Legal Affairs Bureau. Most areas of bilateral defense cooperation in regional contingencies could be planned for if related to the defense of Japan, broadly defined. However, if the two governments seek clear authority for planning even when Japan is not under direct attack, the Cabinet Legal Affairs Bureau may rule any relevant enabling legislation unconstitutional. This action would either precipitate a Diet debate on reinterpreting the constitution to allow collective defense, or force bilateral planning for regional contingencies back into a narrow interpretation of "the defense of Japan" until an actual contingency forced a political decision. Opinon polling suggests that the Japanese public endorses a supporting role for U.S. forces in a regional contingency, but only within the current interpretation of the constitution (which also happens to be the platform of the new populist Democratic Party).

13. These four scenarios are posited to stimulate discussion on the strategic choices available to the United States and Japan, and are not intended to be predictive or inclusive.

However, this essay will focus on scenarios that would test the current alliance structure. One such scenario is a protracted and bloody Korean conflict in which international and domestic pressure is brought to bear on Japan to move beyond rear-area missions into areas that might involve front-line combat defense (for example, air cover in the southern part of the Korean peninsula or antisubmarine warfare/minesweeping operations in Korean waters). Potential repercussions are:

• U.S. bases would become far more important to both the United States and Japan;

• Japan's operational role might have to increase, possibly to include combat activities beyond the defense of the home islands;

• Japan would have to play a larger political role in the region and the United Nations in support of a multinational response to North Korean aggression;

• Japan might be under pressure to share militarily relevant technology with the United States;

• Multilateral security dialogue would be difficult at the height of the conflict but essential to the postwar resolution of peninsular issues;

• Bilateral trade and investment concerns would quickly fade.

The consequences of these pressures for the symmetry/asymmetry balance in various elements of the alliance are illustrated by Figure 3 (compared with the status quo, illustrated by Figure 1). The impact of changes in the elements of the alliance on U.S. and Japanese interests are illustrated by Figure 4 (see next page).

Hostile Sino-U.S. Relations

The April 1996 Security Declaration (resulting from the "Nye Initiative") was designed to improve not only bilateral operational readiness for events on the Korean peninsula but also political readiness to address an increasingly powerful and important China. The United States and Japan were extremely careful not to redefine the alliance or Japan's constitutional framework in any way that

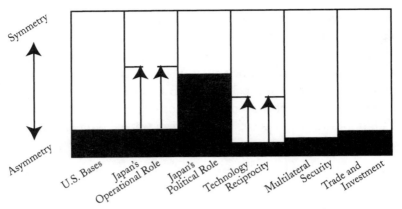

**Figure 3. Pressures on the Alliance in a Protracted
Korean Contingency**

	U.S. — Presence and Influence	Regional Stability	Containment	Economic Access	Burden-Sharing	Deterrence/Capabilities	Global Partnership	JAPAN — Regional Stability	Domestic Stability	Containment	Avoid Conflict	Mercantile Freedom	Global Partnership
Reduce U.S. Bases	-	-	-	-	-	-	-	-	-	-	-	-	-
Increase Japan's Operational Role	+	+	+		+	+	+		-		-	+	
Expand Japan's Political Role						+	+/?			-/?	-/?	+/?	
Technology Reciprocity		+	+	+	+			-/?	-/?			+	
Multilateralism	+/?	+/?				-	+/?	+/?		+/?			
Leverage Security for Trade & Investment	-	-	-	-	-	-	-	-	-	-	-	-	-

**Figure 4. Impact of Restructuring the Alliance for a
Protracted Korean Conflict**

would give the appearance of a strategy of containing China. They understood that as long as Sino-U.S. relations remain nonconfrontational, it would be counterproductive to address many of the asymmetries in the bilateral alliance with Japan.

If, however, China emerged as a political-military competitor to the United States, the impact on the U.S.-Japan alliance would be profound. As long as U.S. forward engagement remained credible, it is unlikely Japan would choose neutrality or appeasement if Beijing challenged U.S. hegemony. A U.S.-provoked confrontation over Taiwan would be more complex from Tokyo's standpoint. In either case, there would be pressure on both the United States and Japan to transform the U.S.-Japan alliance into precisely the instrument of containment that Beijing fears.

In this case:

- U.S. bases would continue to be important to both sides;

- Japan's operational role might have to increase;

- Tokyo's political role would be to complement U.S. strategy in the United Nations and elsewhere;

- Japan would be under pressure to share militarily relevant technology with the United States;

- Multilateral security dialogue could help reduce bipolar tensions and integrate China (though Beijing might resist integration into a U.S.-led system);

- Trade and investment concerns would fade somewhat, though familiar "burden-sharing" arguments might return.

These potential effects are illustrated by Figures 5 and 6 (see next page).

Less Sparkling U.S. Economic Performance

Many of the revisionist arguments in the 1980s against the U.S.-Japan alliance were based on the premise that the Japanese economy was on an upward trajectory while U.S. competitiveness was heading in the opposite direction. The first Clinton administration's Economic Framework approach aimed to address market access problems with a results-oriented focus on specific sectors of the Japanese economy. This approach collapsed in late fall 1995. In fact, bilater-

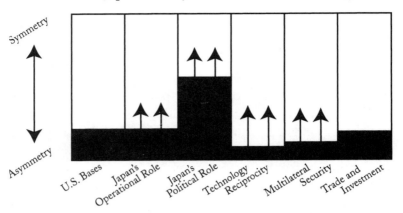

Figure 5. Pressures on the Alliance in a Sino-U.S. Confrontation

	INTERESTS U.S.							JAPAN					
	Presence and Influence	Regional Stability	Containment	Economic Access	Burden-Sharing	Deterrence/Capabilities	Global Partnership	Regional Stability	Domestic Stability	Containment	Avoid Conflict	Mercantile Freedom	Global Partnership
Reduce U.S. Bases	−	−	−	−	−	−	−	−	−	−		−	−
Increase Japan's Operational Role	+	+	+		+	+	+		−	+	−/?	−/?	+
Expand Japan's Political Role		+	+				+		+	−/?	−/?	+	
Technology Reciprocity		−/?		+/?	+/?	+/?		−/?	−/?				+
Multilateralism	+/?	+/?				+/?		+/?	+/?	+/?			
Leverage Security for Trade & Investment	−	−	−	−	−	−	−	−	−	−	−	−	−

Figure 6. Impact of Restructuring the Alliance for a Sino-U.S. Confrontation

al trade tensions ebbed to the point where the April 1996 summit was practically devoid of trade issues.

The Clinton administration's adversarial approach on trade collapsed because of a combination of four factors: 1) sparkling U.S. economic performance contrasted with the dismal post-1992 record in Japan; 2) the growth of strategic alliances between U.S. and Japanese multinationals; 3) the emergence of a "China problem"; and 4) the administration's "no bad news" strategy for the presidential election. Chances are that factors 2) and 3) will continue to mitigate U.S.-Japan trade friction, but factors 1) and 4) could change in ways that either increase trade friction or undermine support for a forward U.S. presence in Japan.

In a post-Korean reunification context in which China is not hostile, the potential for economic issues to affect alliance strategy increases. If U.S. economic performance does not keep up its recent pace, and if, meanwhile, Japan does much better, the alliance asymmetry would come under renewed scrutiny. To maintain domestic support for the alliance and U.S. forward presence, both Washington and Tokyo would feel pressure to redistribute alliance responsibilities, in spite of the possible strategic repercussions.

In particular:

- The United States might reduce the U.S. marine presence on Okinawa or close bases on the main islands of Japan, eliminating rather than withdrawing units to U.S. territory (owing to the loss of Japanese host nation support);

- The Japanese government could feel compelled to increase its military operational role;

- Tokyo might expand its independent political role to keep the United States engaged and hedge against its further withdrawal;

- Washington would seek to obtain access to Japanese military technology—but would have less credibility—and Japanese indigenous weapons development would probably increase;

- Regional multilateral structures could help Japan resist U.S. trade pressure and hedge against further U.S. withdrawal, but might encourage U.S.-Japan political competition;

- The lack of reciprocity in trade and investment would become untenable.

These forces are illustrated in Figures 7 and 8.

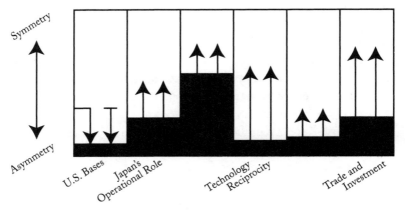

Figure 7. Pressures on the Alliance with Increased Economic Friction

	Presence and Influence	Regional Stability	Containment	Economic Access	Burden-Sharing	Deterrence/Capabilities	Global Partnership	Regional Stability	Domestic Stability	Containment	Avoid Conflict	Mercantile Freedom	Global Partnership
Reduce U.S. Bases	–	–	–	+	+	–	-/?	–	–	–	–	–	-/?
Increase Japan's Operational Role	–	–			+		+		–	+	–		
Expand Japan's Political Role							+/?	+/?	+/?	+/?	-/?		+/?
Technology Reciprocity			+	+	+				-/?			-/?	
Multilateralism	-/?						-/?	+/?	+/?			+/?	
Leverage Security for Trade & Investment	-/?	–	–	+	+	–	-/?	–	–	–	–	–	–

Figure 8. Impact on Restructuring the Alliance in Response to Increased Economic Friction

Michael J. Green

Greater Economic Integration

If an integrationist vision of East Asia's future prevails, and state-to-state relations are marked by a recognized interdependence in which the United States and Japan are equal participants, then the "uncertainty" that is now the raison d'être of the alliance may no longer suffice to sustain it. This could be true even without bilateral trade friction. In this strategic environment, Washington and Tokyo could be compelled to restructure the alliance in fundamental ways:

- The United States could close bases until perhaps only Yokosuka and Kadena remained;[14]

- Japan's operational role could increase incrementally, on the basis of the adoption of the doctrine of collective security (as opposed to the more controversial right to collective defense) and an increase in the trust of neighboring countries;

- Japan's political role could also increase in an environment in which military power mattered less;

- Japan would be under less pressure to provide militarily relevant technology to the United States, but the political taboo against arms exports might have less political salience;

- Multilateral security dialogue could become a new pillar for peace and stability in the region;

- Bilateral trade and investment concerns would fade as the United States and Japan began to focus more on the emerging regional economic powers.

---

14. Yokosuka and Kadena are the "Gibraltars" of U.S. forward air and naval presence in Asia and would arguably have staying power even in an environment of economic integration, growing mutual confidence, and declining budgetary resources.

These effects are illustrated by Figures 9 and 10.

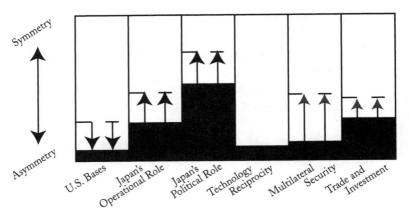

Figure 9. Pressures on the Alliance with Increased Regional Economic Integration

INTERESTS

	U.S.							JAPAN					
	Presence and Influence	Regional Stability	Containment	Economic Access	Burden-Sharing	Deterrence/Capabilities	Global Partnership	Regional Stability	Domestic Stability	Containment	Avoid Conflict	Mercantile Freedom	Global Partnership
Reduce U.S. Bases	-		-/?	-/?	+/?	-/?	+/?	+/?	+/?	-/?		+/?	+/?
Increase Japan's Operational Role				+/?	+/?		+/?			-/?	+/?	+/?	
Expand Japan's Political Role	+/?					+/?	+/?	+/?	-/?			+/?	
Technology Reciprocity	-/?			+/?	+/?	+/?						+/?	
Multilateralism	+/?	+/?				+/?	+	+				+/?	
Leverage Security for Trade & Investment	-	-	-	-/+	-/+	-	-	-	-	-	-	-	-

Figure 10. Impact on Restructuring the Alliance under Increased Economic Integration

Michael J. Green

CONCLUSION

The current configuration of the alliance would probably not survive any of the above scenarios, yet it is equally plausible that the current strategic environment will endure. Moreover, changing the alliance structure in anticipation of any one of these scenarios would likely become a self-fulfilling prophecy. For example:

• Expanding Japan's area of military responsibility to include the Korean Peninsula would undermine U.S.-ROK relations and the consensus that has allowed the first deliberate U.S.-Japan planning for regional contingencies.

• Preparing for a Chinese military threat to the region would turn Beijing from tacit support for the alliance toward hostile intimidation of Tokyo and confrontation with Washington.

• Using the alliance relationship as leverage to force trade and investment results from Tokyo would weaken the alliance—undermining the long-term security of the region—and fail for lack of support from U.S. industry.

• Reducing the U.S. presence in Asia in anticipation of greater economic integration and mutual trust would accelerate rivalry and ultimately undermine mutual trust.

It should not be surprising, therefore, that changes in the U.S.-Japan alliance have always been incremental and rarely structural. Even the April 1996 U.S.-Japan Security Declaration, though billed as a "redefinition" of the alliance, took place within existing structures and only modestly altered the asymmetries in the alliance. In the declaration, the United States and Japan agreed to:

• Return the Okinawan base Futenma MCAS, but without any reduction in U.S. capabilities;

• Review the 1978 guidelines to plan for regional contingencies, but within the current framework of alliance roles and missions and Japan's constitution;

• Consult one another on regional security issues, but without citing a specific threat beyond the Korean peninsula;

• Enhance the exchange of technology and equipment, but without changing Japan's Three Arms Export Principles;

• Develop multilateral security dialogue such as ARF and a Northeast Asian forum.

The incremental effects of the 1996 Declaration are illustrated in Figure 11.

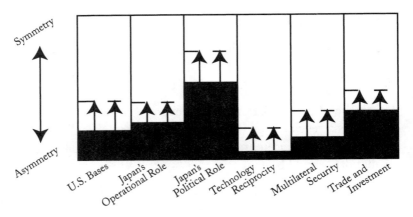

Figure 11. The April 1996 U.S.-Japan Security Declaration

Though incremental, these steps were unprecedented, particularly with regard to regional security cooperation. The "Nye Initiative" and the April 1996 summit introduced into the bilateral security relationship a new confidence that will help both countries adjust to changing situations with more agility than was possible during the Cold War, when there was a simple linear logic to bilateral defense cooperation.

The first example of this new agility was the Okinawa incident. The closer dialogue between the two national security bureaucracies in the months before the rape incident facilitated the implementation of the Special Action Committee on Okinawa (SACO) and the introduction of creative solutions such as the return of Futenma MCAS and the consideration of a floating offshore structure to replace it. Japan's timely political support for the U.S. strike on Iraq in September also represented a new level of trust in the security relationship (despite Tokyo's inability to acknowledge the importance of U.S. bases in the operation).

The April 1996 Security Declaration, SACO, and the review of defense guidelines have all moved the alliance in the right direction and at the right speed. Whether these steps have prepared the alliance for challenges the United States and Japan might face in the next century remains doubtful. But it seems difficult if not impossible for Washington and Tokyo to prepare today for future threats without increasing the likelihood that they will actually materialize.

Rather, a strategy for the alliance over the next few years should aim to achieve greater interoperability and agility, by working within the existing allocation of roles and missions, constitutional framework, and level of political consensus—but by moving ahead whenever possible. Specifically, this translates into ten action points.

1. Complete the Guidelines Review and introduce enabling Diet legislation, joint training, and deliberate operational planning for coordinated responses to regional contingencies (but not restructuring the present division of roles and missions or Japan's constitutional framework in anticipation of the most extreme scenarios).

2. Expand joint R&D, particularly relating to theater missile defense, to develop enabling technologies that contribute to mutual security (but Washington should not insist on reciprocity, regardless of corporate or service interests).

3. Clearly articulate the role that U.S. bases in Japan play in regional and global security to ensure longer-term support for the U.S. presence.

4. Ensure real prior consultation—as opposed to "notification" of Tokyo—on the use of U.S. bases, so that Japan has an equity stake in the U.S. presence.

5. Enter into fuller bilateral dialogue on China, the Middle East, and the Korean peninsula, to include gaming and planning for various contingencies.

6. Hold trilateral defense talks with South Korea that lead to substantive crisis planning (which would be difficult if the structure of bilateral roles and missions were to change).

7 Hold defense talks between the United States, Japan, Russia, and China to build a basis for a future regional multilateral forum (promoting transparency and giving reassurances that the U.S.-Japan alliance is not "anti-Chinese").

8. Increase the level of congressional-Diet exchanges on East Asian security issues.

9. Move toward harmonization of bilateral procurement and enhanced interoperability.

10. Initiate bilateral planning for introduction of theater missile defense systems.

During the Cold War, the U.S.-Japan alliance was primarily a political alliance, represented at the operational level by U.S. bases in Japan. Only in the late 1970s did substantive bilateral defense cooperation begin, and even that was limited to the defense of Japan. The best way to prepare the alliance for the uncertainties of the next century is not to change the superstructure of the alliance, but to fill the operational gaps that remain from the Cold War era, particularly with regard to regional and global security.

The United States and Japan cannot rely on a static alliance to remain strong and vital. The alliance must be steadily redefined from the inside out if it is to be agile enough to protect the interests of both partners in a changing and unpredictable strategic environment.

Japanese Security Policy

Mike M. Mochizuki

INTRODUCTION

OVER THE LAST SEVEN years, external developments have provoked a lively debate in Japan about the country's role in international affairs, inducing incremental, but nonetheless significant, changes in its diplomatic and security policies. The end of the Cold War brought both cheer and anxiety in Tokyo: although the possibility of Soviet-American nuclear crossfire disappeared, the collapse of the Soviet Union raised questions about the international order that had benefited Japan so enormously in both economic and security terms. The Persian Gulf crisis of 1990–91 invoked doubts about Japan's "checkbook diplomacy" and "one-country pacifism." Tensions over North Korea's nuclear program reminded Japanese leaders that Japan would inevitably become involved in a crisis on the Korean peninsula. China's nuclear tests and its military exercises in the Taiwan Strait suggested not only that China might emerge as a security threat to Japan but also that a Sino-American confrontation over Taiwan would force Japan to make hard choices. The clumsy response to the Kobe earthquake and the shock of the Aum Shinrikyo cult's poison gas attack in the Tokyo subway (both of which occurred in 1995) convinced many Japanese that the state needed to improve its ability to manage crises. The 1997 hostage crisis in Peru, in which several Japanese diplomats were held, forced Japanese to think more seriously about security issues. And finally, the September 1995 Okinawa rape incident stirred up local hostility to the U.S. military presence on the island and caused a sharp drop in public support for the security relationship with the United States.

[25]

Though none of these events has precipitated a major shift in Japan's strategic posture, together they have stimulated soul-searching about national identity. The current strategic debate and the incremental policy changes might eventually yield a new Japan that will respond differently to future external challenges than the Japan of the Cold War years.

THE STRATEGIC DEBATE

The sharp ideological conflict over security policy that existed during much of the Cold War era has faded. There is now in Japan a broad-based consensus that supports the following propositions: 1) maintenance of the security alliance with the United States; 2) U.S. military engagement in Asia-Pacific; 3) the constitutional legitimacy of the Self-Defense Forces (JSDF) and the right to individual self-defense; 4) the three nonnuclear principles, namely, not to manufacture, possess, or bring in nuclear weapons; and 5) the rising importance for Japanese interests of East Asian economic development and security stability. What is primarily being debated now are specific issues within these general parameters. These issues include the following:

- *The Constitution:* Should the constitution be revised or reinterpreted, and in what way?

- *Terms of the U.S.-Japan alliance:* What role should Japan play in U.S. military operations beyond the defense of Japan? What should the size and character of the U.S. military presence in Japan be? How much and what kind of diplomatic autonomy should Japan have in relation to the United States?

- *Japan Self-Defense Forces:* What size, structure, and capabilities should the Self-Defense Forces have in the post–Cold War era, and what role should the forces play beyond the defense of Japan?

- *Nuclear policy:* In what manner should Japan promote nuclear nonproliferation and nuclear disarmament? Should Japan continue to rely on U.S. extended nuclear deterrence? What kind of nuclear energy policy should Japan pursue?

• *Multilateral security:* To what extent should Japan emphasize the building of multilateral security institutions?

• *Economic interdependence and security:* To what extent can economic interdependence mitigate geopolitical suspicions and promote regional stability?

• *History:* How should Japan deal with the issue of its militarist past?

• *Korea:* How should Japan deal with the problem of a divided Korea and the possibility of a reunited Korea?

• *China:* How should Japan deal with the rise of China and the Taiwan question?

Although mainstream views on each of these questions vary widely, opinion tends to cluster around two conceptions of national identity: Japan as a "normal country" and Japan as a "civilian power." The "civilian power" perspective probably still commands more support in the general public, reflecting the persistence of pacifistic norms. But international developments during the last seven years have significantly increased the influence of the "normal country" perspective. Recent opinion polls conducted by the *Yomiuri Shimbun* show that over half the population now favors revising the constitution; a decade ago, the issue of constitutional revision was essentially taboo. And in April 1996, the influential organization of business executives Keizai Doyukai endorsed reinterpretation of the constitution so that Japan could exercise its right to collective self-defense.

In addition to these two mainstream perspectives, there are those who want Japan to become a "pacifist state" in a stricter sense and those who would like it to be an "autonomous great power." Both options lie outside the general policy consensus that exists today. Barring a radical change in the international environment, neither the "pacifist state" nor the "autonomous great power" view of Japan will become the predominant perspective. For the foreseeable future, the salient debate for policy will be the competition between the "normal country" and "civilian power" visions. But the other two visions will matter politically, in that they affect the relative influence of the two mainstream schools of thought.

What follows is a brief synopsis of the main positions found in each of these four opinion clusters. This summary will map each of the clusters according to the specific issues identified above, but the descriptions are not entirely comparable because one opinion cluster may not have as detailed views on a particular subject as another.

The "Normal Country" Perspective

The vision of Japan as a "normal country" has two versions: one based on "collective security" centered on the United Nations, the other on "collective defense" anchored in the alliance with the United States. Reform politician Ichiro Ozawa supports the "collective security" version by emphasizing the common ground that the Japanese constitution, the U.S.-Japan Security Treaty, and the U.N. Charter share. Without revising the constitution, he believes that the Japanese Self-Defense Forces can and should move beyond their current "exclusive defense strategy" and participate in U.N. peacekeeping activities on both an ad hoc basis and as part of a U.N. standing force. He suggests that Japan could even participate in U.N. "preventive or enforcement measures" under Chapter 7 of the U.N. Charter. What the present constitution prohibits is "the use of military force abroad by the Japanese government *based on its own decision*" (italics Ozawa's).[1]

Although Ozawa was the original popularizer of the "normal country" concept, most Japanese analysts who subscribe to a "realist" view of international politics question Ozawa's expectations for a U.N.-centered collective security system and stress instead the concept of "collective defense" for reinvigorating Japan's alliance with the United States.[2] This view of Japanese normalization focuses on deter-

---

1. Ozawa, *Blueprint for a New Japan* (Tokyo: Kodansha, 1994), pp. 106–107, 109–111, 119–121.

2. Some of the prominent Japanese realists are Masamichi Inoki (professor emeritus at Kyoto University and adviser to the Research Institute for Peace and Security), Kenichi Ito (president of the Japan Forum on International Relations), Shinichi Kitaoka (professor at Rikkyo University), Yoshihisa Komori (special editorial writer, *Sankei Shimbun*), Satoshi Morimoto (senior researcher at the Nomura Research Institute and former

rence, crisis management, and balance of power. Nevertheless, since Ozawa and traditional realists share a commitment to enhance Japan's military role in international security, the following summary of the "normal country" perspective treats the two views together except the points on which they disagree.

Constitution

Ozawa argues that the current constitution permits Japan to participate in virtually all U.N. collective security operations, if the forces are under U.N. command. Most other "realists" believe that the government should change its current interpretation of the constitution (and eventually move to amend the constitution formally) so that Japan can exercise its right to collective self-defense as well as its right to individual self-defense.[3]

U.S.-Japan Alliance and U.S. Forces

Notwithstanding all the defense burden-sharing efforts of the Japanese government, alliances face their greatest tests during crises. No amount of "host-nation support" or checkbook diplomacy will satisfy the United States if American lives are being sacrificed in an East Asia contingency—e.g., in Korea or over Taiwan—that is

---

Ministry of Foreign Affairs official), Masashi Nishihara (professor at the National Defense Academy), Okazaki Hisahiko (former Japanese ambassador to Saudi Arabia and Thailand), Seizaburo Sato (professor at the Saitama University Graduate School and research director of the Institute for International Policy Studies), Toshiyuki Shikata (professor at Teikyo University and retired lieutenant general of the Ground Self-Defense Force), Tadae Takubo (professor at Kyorin University), Akihiko Tanaka (professor at Tokyo University), and Akio Watanabe (professor at Aoyama Gakuin University).

3. Recent articles advocating constitutional reinterpretation include: Inoki Masamichi, "Kuso-teki heiwashugi ni ketsubetsu o," *This Is Yomiuri*, July 1996, pp. 128–137; Sase Masamori, "'Shudan-teki jieiken' kaishaku no kai," *Voice*, July 1996, pp. 128–149; Shiina Motoo and Okazaki Hisahiko, "Shúdan-teki jieiken rongi o nigeru na," *Chúó Kóron*, July 1996, pp. 62–69; Okazaki Hisahiko, "Japan Should Awake to Right to Collective Self-defense," *The Daily Yomiuri*, July 4, 1994; and Komori Yoshihisa, "Hemmu jóyaku wa iranai," *Voice*, May 1996, pp. 186–195.

A group within Ozawa's New Frontier Party known as the New Frontier Party Security Diet Members' League (Shinshintó Anzen Hoshó Gi-in Renmei Yúshi) has proposed such a change in constitutional interpretation in its draft policy entitled "Security Policy Outline for the New Century: New Thinking on Security and Defense." Because of strong opposition from some segments of the New Frontier Party, this policy outline has not become part of the party's official platform.

critical to Japanese interests while Japan stands idly by because of its constitutional constraints. Therefore, the "normal country" advocates argue that Japan should at least provide rear-area support for U.S. troops during a regional military contingency. Some would ultimately like Japanese soldiers to stand shoulder to shoulder with U.S. forces in the defense of common interests.[4]

Most would like to have the United States maintain its military presence in Japan at close to current levels, and they are willing to defer to the Pentagon regarding what forces are required. Hosting U.S. forces is the best guarantee of America's security commitment to Japan and the most effective way to ensure U.S. strategic engagement in East Asia. But a few are beginning to favor a reduction in the Marine Corps presence in Okinawa and an augmentation of naval and air forces.

Japan should play a role in American power balancing in East Asia analogous to the role that Britain plays for the United States in Europe—serving as America's most reliable regional partner—the realists say.

Self-Defense Forces
There is no need to acquire power projection capabilities, although Japan should upgrade its air and missile defense and its intelligence-gathering systems. A few advocate the acquisition of long-range transport capabilities for peacekeeping missions and a small aircraft carrier for air defense.

Nuclear Policy
Japan should continue to rely on U.S. extended nuclear deterrence, a doctrine that allows Japan to sustain its three nonnuclear principles. Japan should work with the United States to strengthen the nuclear nonproliferation regime, but also continue to develop its plutonium program for long-term energy security.

---

4. Shikata Toshiyuki, *Kyoku-to yuji* [Far East Crisis] (Tokyo: Kuresuto Sha, 1996), and Okazaki Hisahiko, "Japan Should Awake to Right to Collective Self-defense".

Multilateral Security

Ozawa has stated that, through multilateral diplomacy, Japan should "develop a new security framework that can respond to the power vacuum that would be left by an American withdrawal."[5] But for most "collective defense" realists, rather than developing a regional multilateral security framework to prepare for a possible U.S. military withdrawal, Japan should strengthen the U.S.-Japan alliance to ensure the continuation of America's security involvement in the Asia-Pacific region. The bilateral alliance is the most important pillar of regional security; multilateral security dialogues and institutions can only be supplemental.

Economic Interdependence

For "normal country" advocates, growing economic interdependence is insufficient to promote regional peace. In fact, economic growth in the context of this interdependence is likely to provide East Asian states the resources to enhance their military capabilities. Therefore the development and maintenance of a stable balance of power is essential to regional security. Asia-Pacific Economic Cooperation (APEC) may help to sustain regional economic growth and promote liberalization, but its contribution to security is limited.

History

Ozawa acknowledges the need to deal more forthrightly with Japan's militarist past in order to win the trust of other Asian states, but he also stresses the importance of having a balanced view of history (noting the positive role Japan has played in the region).[6] Others feel that the historical question persists primarily because some Japanese politicians, journalists, and even officials "tip off" Koreans and Chinese about "off-the-record" remarks or internal developments so as to provoke an outcry. Japan must transcend the "history question" in developing a forward-looking policy toward Asia. Ultimately, greater objectivity is needed in analyzing Japan's historical role in Asia. Equating imperialist Japan with Nazi Germany is misguided and unfair, they say.

---

5. Ozawa, *Blueprint for a New Japan*, pp. 135–137.
6. Ibid. pp. 128–129.

Korea

Japan should be prepared to cooperate militarily with the United States and South Korea during a Korean crisis. It should also promote security cooperation with the United States to strengthen deterrence against a North Korean attack. Japan would, of course, prefer a reunited Korea that has good relations with both Japan and the United States to one that is either neutral or aligned with China. But a reunited Korea is not that problematic, whatever its strategic posture, as long as Japan's alliance with the United States is solid.

China/Taiwan

According to the realists, the best way to ensure stability in the Asia-Pacific region is to balance a rising China with a strong U.S.-Japan alliance. Balancing China, however, does not mean pursuing a containment strategy vis-à-vis China similar to the one pursued against the Soviet Union. China is more an irredentist power than an expansionist power with grand imperial designs like the old Soviet Union. If nationalism drives China to become more assertive territorially, its targets are likely to be limited to Taiwan, the South China Sea, and possibly Siberia. As long as China's growing military power can be balanced by a robust U.S.-Japan alliance (if need be, through a coalition with other states on China's periphery), then both Japan and the United States should have no qualms about assisting China's economic development and its integration into the world economy.[7] But in a Sino-American military confrontation over Taiwan, for example, Japan has no choice but to support the United States.[8]

---

7. While acknowledging that Japan is "not in a position to interfere in resolving the Taiwan question," Okazaki Hisahiko asserts that if China and the United States were to collide over this issue, Japan has no choice but to cooperate with the United States in order to sustain the bilateral alliance. Okazaki Hisahiko, "Ajia no ashita to Nichi-Bei domei," *This Is Yomiuri*, December 1996, p. 209.

8. Ibid.

Mike M. Mochizuki

The "Civilian Power" Perspective

An *Asahi Shimbun* journalist, Yoichi Funabashi, first introduced the concept of "civilian power" to a Japanese audience.[9] Rather than turning Japan into an "ordinary" country, Funabashi and those who share his basic outlook argue that Japan should build constructively on its militarist past and strive to internationalize its current norms about security and the use of military force. Increasing economic interdependence and the end of the Cold War will attenuate the need to rely on traditional "balance of power" approaches to security, and an opportunity to cultivate "cooperative" approaches to security will instead emerge. Consequently policymakers should place greater emphasis on nonmilitary and multilateral means to enhance international security.[10] The following summarizes the "civilian power" position on specific issues.

Constitution

Instead of viewing the postwar constitution as impeding a more prominent Japanese role in international affairs, the Japanese should see it as an enunciation of ideals that all states should work toward, ideals that Japan should take the lead in promoting. Therefore, "civilian power" advocates argue that the constitution should be preserved, not amended or reinterpreted.

---

9. Yoichi Funabashi first referred to the "global civilian power" concept in two English-language articles: "Japan and the New World Order," *Foreign Affairs*, vol. 70, no. 5 (Winter 1991/92), pp. 58–74; and "Japan and America: Global Partners," *Foreign Policy*, no. 86 (Spring 1992), pp. 24–39. He developed the concept in more detail in his book *Nihon no taigai kōsō: Reisen go no bijon o kaku* (Tokyo: Iwanami Shoten, 1993). Funabashi acknowledges his debt to Hanns W. Maull for coining the term "civilian power" in the article "Germany and Japan: The New Civilian Powers," *Foreign Affairs*, vol. 69, no. 5 (Winter 1990/91), pp. 91–106.

10. Japanese commentators who generally support the substance of Funabashi's "global civilian power" concept include Hisayoshi Ina (editorial writer for *Nihon Keizai Shimbun*), Terumasa Nakanishi (professor at Kyoto University), Shunji Taoka (editorial writer for the *Asahi Shimbun*), and Jitsuro Terashima (director of the Washington, D.C., office of *Mitsui Bussan*).

U.S.-Japan Alliance and U.S. Forces

In this era of transition and uncertainty, the security alliance between Japan and the United States must be maintained. But analysts in the "civilian power" opinion cluster differ among themselves about how the security relationship should evolve.

Some would like the security relationship to move away from permanent U.S. military forces stationed on Japanese territory (*jóji chúryú naki Ampó*).[11] Others argue that without military bases in Japan, the United States would have little incentive to continue its defense commitments to Japan. Nevertheless, they still feel that the number of U.S. troops and bases in Japan should be reduced to lighten the burden on various local communities, especially Okinawa.[12]

Although many recoil at the thought of Japan's cooperating militarily with the United States in a Far East crisis beyond the homeland, some believe that the Japanese Self-Defense Forces should support U.S. military operations in regional contingencies—within the constraints of the constitution. If a danger were to emerge in the region critically affecting Japan's defense, then Japan could cooperate with U.S. forces as an extension of the right to individual self-defense. But the iron law holds: Japan must renounce the use of military force in foreign countries.[13]

Some would like Japan to assert its own diplomatic positions on important issues such as relations with China, Taiwan policy, and nuclear nonproliferation—even though they might be at odds with U.S. policy. They do not prescribe an open break with the United States, but they do foresee the diplomatic independence that Germany has exhibited in recent years.

---

11. Taoka Shunji, *Senryaku no jóken* (Tokyo: Yúhi-sha, 1994), pp. 264–270; and Terashima Jitsuro, "'Shin-bei nyu-a' no sogo senryaku o motomete," *Chuo koron*, March 1996, pp. 32–35.

12. Maehara Seiji, "Nihon ni dekiru bóei kyóryoku," *Voice*, October 1996, pp. 178–187, and "Japan's Security Policy: A Time for Realism," *The Japan Digest*, December 11, 1996, p. 5. A member of the Japanese House of Representatives, Representative Maehara chairs the Democratic Party (Minshutó) Security Affairs subcommittee.

13. Miyazawa Kiichi, "Kokumin no mae de yuji rongi o" [interview], *Asahi Shimbun*, May 3, 1996.

Self-Defense Forces

The JSDF should stick to as "exclusively defensive" military posture and refrain from acquiring military systems that can project power
or threaten other countries. The JSDF should participate in U.N.
peacekeeping operations in noncombatant roles. It should not,
however, join peacemaking or peace-enforcement missions that
would require the use of force overseas.

Nuclear Policy

As the only country to suffer from a nuclear attack, Japan should
become more vigorous about preventing nuclear proliferation and
supporting nuclear arms control and disarmament. Japan should not
be shy about criticizing China for conducting nuclear tests and for
building a nuclear arsenal. A few in this cluster contemplate moving Japan out from under the U.S. nuclear umbrella in order to give
its nonnuclear policy greater moral force, especially vis-à-vis China.
At the same time, many favor plutonium reprocessing as part of Japan's
long-term energy strategy.

Multilateral Security

Drawing on the lessons of the premature dissolution of the Anglo-
Japanese alliance in 1922, the U.S.-Japan alliance should not be replaced
with the untested alternative of a multilateral security arrangement in the Asia Pacific.[14] Still, the U.S.-centered bilateral security arrangements that were established to deal principally with the
Soviet threat are no longer sufficient to manage the "plural and broadly defined threats" of the post–Cold War era. Multilateral security
dialogues are increasingly necessary to foster mutual trust through
a variety of communication channels.[15]

---

14. Yoichi Funabashi, *Asia Pacific Fusion: Japan's Role in APEC* (Washington, DC:
Institute for International Economics, 1995), pp. 252–253.
15. Ina Hisayoshi, "Kokusai kankei no atarashii tenkai to Nichi-Bei anzen hosho taisei,"
Gaiko Forum, kinkyu zōkan - June 1996, pp. 109–111; and Hisayoshi Ina, *A New Multi-
lateral Approach for the Pacific: Beyond the Bilateral Security Network* (Washington, DC:
The Foreign Policy Institute Papers, 1993).

Economic Interdependence

Although the Asia-Pacific region lacks treaty institutions such as NATO or the European Union (EU), and suffers from the absence of mature civil societies in many countries, and manifests large differences in income and cultural traditions, the focus on economic growth throughout the region will over time ameliorate traditional geopolitical suspicions. In this context, APEC can play a decisive role in fostering a sense of community in the region.[16]

History

Japan still has not adequately dealt with its militarist past. Only after fully acknowledging the atrocities that the Japanese military committed in Asia during the Second World War will Japan gain the trust of its Asian neighbors, "civilian power" supporters say. Greater school and public education is necessary in Japan on this issue. Clearing the historical issue is a precondition for Japan's assuming a broader political-security role in the region.

Korea

Japan should put relations with South Korea on firmer ground by dealing more effectively with the historical issues and by absorbing more imports from South Korea. But at the same time, Japan should facilitate North Korea's incorporation into the regional economic community as a way of defusing military tensions on the Korean peninsula. The best way to ensure good relations with a reunified Korea is to play a constructive role in the reunification process.

China/Taiwan

To develop a stable and cooperative balance among the United States, Japan, and China, America and Japan should move quickly to integrate China into the regional and international community. Otherwise Beijing will view the U.S.-Japan alliance as a means to contain China.[17] Therefore Japan should continue to facilitate China's

---

16. Funabashi, *Asian Pacific Fusion*, pp. 246–251.

17. Yoichi Funabashi, "Bridging Asia's Economics-Security Gap," *Survival*, vol. 36, no. 4 (Winter 1996–97), pp. 112–113.

economic development and its accession to the World Trade Organization.

Some support a strict policy of noninterference on the Taiwan question—even if China and the United States confront each other on this issue.

The "Pacifist State" Perspective

Unlike the "unarmed neutralists" of old, the leading commentators who want Japan to be a "pacifist state" now recognize Japan's right to defend itself and acknowledge the beneficial effects of the U.S.-Japan security treaty, especially the clauses on economic cooperation and the settlement of disputes by peaceful means. They even admit that the treaty has helped to restrain Japanese rearmament and to make other Asian states receptive to Japan's emergence as a regional economic leader. But they criticize reliance on the security treaty with the United States to reassure the region about Japanese intentions. It is far better to reaffirm unequivocally Japan's status as a pacifist state and resist U.S. pressures to "militarize" the alliance. The "pacifist state" view on specific issues is as follows.

Constitution
The constitution should be neither revised nor reinterpreted. By preserving its "peace constitution," Japan should act as a "conscientious objector" nation, one that contributes to international society in exclusively nonmilitary ways.

U.S.-Japan Alliance and U.S. Forces
There is ultimately a tension between the U.S.-Japan alliance and the creation of inclusive cooperative security arrangements. Therefore, in the view of the pacifists, Japan and the United States should amicably scale back the military aspects of the alliance and recast the relationship as a political, economic, and cultural partnership. Over time, U.S. military forces should be removed from Japanese territory. Only by transforming the relationship with the United States in this manner can Japan pursue a peace strategy as a truly sovereign nation.

Self-Defense Forces

The Self-Defense Forces should be transformed from its current structure as a traditional military force into a security organization similar to the police or the coast guard. This "minimum defensive force" (*saishogen bógyóryoku*) would be a "democratized" and open unit. Its aim would be to protect the lives and property of Japanese citizens, and its geographic scope would be strictly limited to Japan's land, airspace, and territorial waters.[18] Japan should refrain from acquiring weapons that can be used to attack other countries, from deploying military forces overseas, and from exercising the right to collective self-defense. The JSDF should reduce its ground forces by half and scale back advanced weapon systems like the Aegis naval systems and P-3C antisubmarine warfare aircraft.[19]

To contribute actively to international peace, some favor establishing a separate Peace Support Corps (*Heiwa Shi-en Tai*), limited to humanitarian and economic operations. Pacifists say the use of military force or the deployment of armed peacekeepers is unlikely to be effective in resolving regional conflicts, and point out that such operations may even aggravate the problem.

Nuclear Policy

According to the "pacifist state" vision, Japan should adhere strictly to its three nonnuclear principles and codify these principles into law. It should promote the cause of nuclear disarmament by terminating its reliance on the U.S. nuclear umbrella. Japan should also end its plutonium recycling policy to allay suspicions about Japan's nuclear intentions.

Multilateral Security

In place of the security alliance, Japan should take the lead in developing a multilateral, collective, and cooperative security system for the Asia-Pacific region that has the ability to impose sanctions and perform peacekeeping functions.

---

18. Kozeki Shoichi et. al., "Ajia-Taiheiyo Chi-iki Ampo o koso suru," *Sekai*, December 1994, pp. 25–28.

19. Asahi Shimbun Ronsetsu I-inshitsu (ed.), *Kokusai Kyóryoku to Kempó: Asahi Shimbun wa teigen suru* (Tokyo: Asahi Shimbunsha, 1995), pp. 39–46.

Mike M. Mochizuki

Economic Interdependence

As economic interdependence increases among East Asian states, a sense of regional community will inevitably develop, obviating the need to rely on geopolitical alliances to preserve security. At the same time, Japan should work with countries in the region to reduce the negative environmental consequences of economic development.

History

If Japan is to be trusted by its neighbors, it must address more sincerely the legacy of its militarist past. Unfortunately, many of the pro-defense politicians and opinion leaders are the least willing to admit to the wrongs that Japan committed against other Asians. Until Japan can clear the hurdle of the historical question, revising the constitution to clarify Japan's international role will be misconstrued and may even become a destabilizing factor in the region.

Korea

With the U.S.–North Korea Agreed Framework and the improvement in relations between China and South Korea, the basic trend is positive for defusing tensions on the Korean peninsula. Therefore, according to the pacifists, Japan should not undermine this trend by expanding the military dimension of its relationship with the United States. Although its nuclear program is worrisome, North Korea poses no immediate threat to Japanese security.

China/Taiwan

China is modernizing its military, but its military power is not directed at Japan, and it will take some time before China becomes a military threat to the region. In the meantime, Japan should continue to support China's economic development and its integration into the regional and global community and encourage China to become a force for peace. Japan should not be shy about criticizing China for its nuclear tests and even using foreign economic assistance as leverage.

The best way to deal with China is to develop multilateral security institutions like the Association of Southeast Asian Nations (ASEAN) Regional Forum and to deepen the dialogue with China. So far, multilateral approaches have helped to manage territorial disputes in the South China Sea. Redefining the U.S.-Japan alliance so that Japan's security role is expanded geographically will only alarm the Chinese and undermine efforts to cultivate a cooperative security regime.

The best way to promote peace across the Taiwan Strait is to encourage deeper economic links between mainland China and Taiwan. Japan, however, should refrain from intervening politically or militarily on this issue, according to pacifist advocates.

The "Autonomous Great Power" Perspective

Like the "pacifist state" advocates, proponents of the "autonomous great power" vision would like Japan to pursue a strategy more independent of the United States. Rather than adhering to the constitution, which they see as imposed by an external power, they favor rewriting the constitution so that it better reflects indigenous values. Although in the past "great power nationalists" supported the acquisition of nuclear weapons, few in this cluster openly recommend nuclear acquisition today. In fact, they hardly say anything at all about the details of military policy. But they do criticize the bilateral security treaty and the U.S. military presence in Japan as primarily serving American interests and not those of Japan. In recent years, the main theme of "autonomous great power" supporters has been the decline of the United States and the West and the rise of Asia. Rather than blindly following the American lead or Western models, Japan should replant its roots in Asia.[20] This "Asianist" evolution of "great power nationalism" has meant that advocates are much less specific about concrete security policy questions than their counterparts in the other opinion clusters, as is evident in the following summary.

Constitution
The constitution, which was imposed by the United States, should be revised so that Japan can take greater responsibility for its own defense.

---

20. Ishihara Shintaro and Mahathir, *"No" to ieru Ajia* (Tokyo: Kobunsha, 1994).

U.S.-Japan Alliance and U.S. Forces

The bilateral security framework should ultimately be revised to make the relationship more equal and symmetrical. Japan should change the view that U.S. forces are in Japan to defend Japan. The reality is that U.S. forces are in Japan to promote U.S. strategic interests beyond Japan. The notion that Japan is a free rider of U.S. security policy is therefore a myth. The United States has worked to keep Japan from becoming a truly sovereign nation.

Many favor a reduction of U.S. bases throughout Japan, not just Okinawa. For example, Shintaro Ishihara has called for a return of the Yokota Air Force Base as the price for sustained Japanese support for the bilateral alliance.[21]

Self-Defense Forces

"Autonomous great power" proponents believe that, at the very least, the JSDF should be able to participate fully in U.N. peacekeeping forces. However, to defuse the concerns of Asian countries, Japan should be transparent about the structure of its military forces.[22] According to this cluster, it is of paramount importance for the Japanese military to gain full legitimacy, and for defense planning to be focused on ensuring Japanese security, rather than bogged down in esoteric constitutional questions.

Nuclear Policy

Since the end of the Cold War, most in this opinion cluster no longer advocate the acquisition of nuclear weapons.[23] However, they are certainly aware that, with its technical know-how and plutonium reprocessing facilities, Japan could acquire nuclear weapons in short order.

Multilateral Security

The world is moving toward a tripolar structure centered on North America, Europe, and East Asia. The notion that Japan should play

---

21. Ishihara Shintaro, *Kaku are sokoku* (Tokyo: Kobunsha, 1994), pp. 137–142.

22. Ibid., pp. 108–109.

23. One of the few exceptions is a young military commentator, Hyozo Nisohara. See his "Nippon retto kaku heibi keikaku," *Shokun*, October 1996, pp. 202–213.

a mediating role between East and West is naive. Japan should clearly articulate its position of being a member of the "East." Although relations with the United States will remain important, it is much more natural for Japan to put greater emphasis on its relations with Asia.[24]

Economic Interdependence and Security
Japan's primary mission should be the promotion of Asia's economic development, and it can contribute to regional stability by creating a yen-based economic sphere.[25]

History
Japan should not be preoccupied with the historical issue. In fact, the Tokyo war crimes trial version of the Pacific war is inaccurate and biased against Japan. Reports of Japanese atrocities in World War II are grossly exaggerated. Moreover, many of the countries in East Asia are now willing to put aside the past and are looking to Japan for more international leadership.[26]

Relations with East Asia
Advocates of a "great power" Japan offer very little in the way of concrete measures for dealing with either Korea or China. Most write vaguely about deepening Japan's relations with the East Asian countries by stressing the common Toyo (Eastern) philosophy and civilization they share. A few discuss the need to "neutralize" a reunited Korea in cooperation with the other great powers (China, Russia, and the United States).

---

24. Shintaro and Mahathir, *"No" to ieru Ajia*, pp. 44–45.
25. Ibid., pp. 224–231.
26. Watanabe Shoichi and Komuro Naoki, *Onozukara kuni o tsubusu no ka* (Tokyo: Tokuma Shoten, 1993).

Mike M. Mochizuki

DYNAMICS OF THE STRATEGIC DEBATE

Four general points can be made about this strategic debate. First, while the influence of the "normal country" perspective has grown, the "civilian power" view still commands enough support to obstruct Japan's "normalization" process and ensure an incremental pace of change in Japanese security policy. Much of the Japanese population continues to have an aversion to the military. Not only does the newly formed Democratic Party back the "civilian power" perspective (and to a significant extent even the "pacifist state" view), but sizable groups in both the Liberal Democratic Party (LDP) and the New Frontier Party (NFP) embrace this dovish vision. The complex web of competing bureaucratic interests, as well as the weakness of the prime minister as an agent of change, favors the "civilian power" perspective by slowing down the expansion of Japan's security role.

Second, the relative influence of the "normal country" and "civilian power" opinion clusters will depend on the evolution of the international environment. What will matter most is the balance between the level of security threat to Japan and the robustness of America's defense commitment. If the environment becomes more threatening to Japan while the U.S. security commitment to Japan continues as before, then support for the "normal country" perspective will increase: the Japanese people will become more convinced of their nation's security vulnerability and the need to strengthen the alliance with the United States. But if the threat increases while the U.S. commitment decreases, Japan may move beyond the "normal country" perspective to the "autonomous great power perspective." Or Japan could even go in the opposite direction of appeasing the threat by adhering to a "civilian power" stance or a more pacifistic version.

If the environment moves in a more benign direction (such as a reduction of tensions in Korea or across the Taiwan Strait), however, then the influence of the "civilian power" perspective will grow. The public would see no need to broaden Japan's military role beyond defense of the home islands, nor to strengthen the military dimension of the U.S.-Japan security relationship.

[43]

Third, the "normal country" and "civilian power" visions both have their deficiencies. Although the "normal country" view may have a more realistic grasp of regional security trends, its treatment of the history question complicates Japan's ability to assume a broader security role without exacerbating regional tensions. The legacy of Japan's colonization of Korea, its aggression against China, and its war with the United States still makes Asia uncomfortable about Japan. Conversely, while the "civilian power" vision may create a Japan that could be more active in the security realm without destabilizing the region, it expects too much from economic interdependence and multilateral security dialogues for dealing with geopolitical tensions.

Fourth, the "pacifist state" and "autonomous great power" visions are declining in influence, but they still attract more attention in Japan than their influence would warrant, because of Japanese frustrations about relations with the United States. This is particularly true of the "autonomous great power" vision. The role of these two opinion clusters on policy should not be entirely dismissed. The overlap between the "civilian power" and "pacifist state" views and between the "normal country" and "autonomous great power" views is considerable and has probably increased over time.

The "civilian power" and the "pacifist state" opinion clusters now agree not only about the constitutional legitimacy of the Self-Defense Forces and the benefits of the U.S.-Japan Security Treaty, but also about the need for (and inevitability of) a reduction in U.S. forces in Japan. The "normal country" and "great power" advocates now agree about the need to revise or reinterpret the constitution. As support for nuclear weapons has waned in the "great power" group, the gap between them regarding military policy has narrowed. Consequently the two extreme views may play a more prominent role in the competition between the two mainstream views. The "normal country" and "great power" advocates could cooperate more, on a political level, to promote their common agenda, and the "civilian power" and "pacifist state" proponents could do the same.

Mike M. Mochizuki

JAPANESE POLITICS AND THE STATE

From a domestic point of view, how the above strategic debate influences the world of concrete policy will depend largely on party and bureaucratic politics.

Party Politics

When the ruling Liberal Democratic Party split in 1993, Japanese commentators heralded the end of the so-called 1955 system. Under this system, the LDP had maintained political hegemony, while the competition (and later collusion) between the LDP and the Japan Socialist Party (JSP) shaped much of the dynamics of party and parliamentary politics. In reality, the events of the last three years amounted more to a culmination of the post-1955 system than to its collapse. By uniting to form the LDP in 1955, the conservatives in Japan were pursuing their political objective of containing, taming, dividing, and ultimately incorporating the political left led by the JSP. The conservatives succeeded in this hegemonic program all too well. From a historical perspective, the most significant development of the past few years was not the temporary ouster of the LDP from power but the demise of the JSP as a political force. The end of the Cold War and the decline of socialism as an ideology dissolved the glue that helped to keep the factionalized LDP together. Conservative reformers outmaneuvered the JSP and trapped the party into acquiescing to an electoral reform that certainly spelled the party's annihilation.

As the sharp ideological conflict over security policy faded into a broad public consensus, policy positions have waned as a decisive factor in party affiliation and alignments. Much more important now are calculations about electoral and office opportunities. And despite the overhaul of the electoral system in 1994, debates about policy are no more important than before in electoral competition and performance.

The LDP and NFP are virtually indistinguishable in terms of positions on foreign and security policy. Advocates of both the "normal country" and the "civilian power" visions reside in both parties. At present, differences within these two parties perhaps mat-

[45]

ter more politically than the differences between them. Ozawa and his colleagues in the NFP were unable to get the party to endorse a platform along the lines of the "normal country" vision because of strong internal opposition. Prime Minister Ryutaro Hashimoto has been constrained from pushing more aggressively on defense cooperation with the United States not only because his LDP must rely on the surviving Social Democrats for votes in the upper house, but also because he faces resistance from within his own party. These intraparty divisions discourage an open partisan debate about foreign and security policies, as was evident in the tone of the October 1996 election campaign. The Democratic Party is somewhat more cohesive, but even here members range from "civilian power" to "pacifist state" proponents. Perhaps only the Japan Communist Party (JCP) has a coherent and consistent position (terminating the security relationship with the United States and pursuing an autonomous diplomatic policy), but its views are very much the minority.

Although Japanese politics is now in a confusing transitional phase, one can still draw several tentative inferences about the connection between party politics and strategic policy. First, most Diet members, irrespective of party affiliation, fall within the general policy parameters noted earlier: maintenance of the U.S.-Japan alliance, U.S. military engagement in the Asia-Pacific region, the legitimacy of the Self-Defense Forces, the three nonnuclear principles, and the growing importance of East Asian economic development and security stability for Japanese interests.

Second, despite the cross-cutting cleavages between parties and policy position, an international crisis—e.g., over Korea, Taiwan, or relations with the United States—could provoke a political realignment around the different strategic visions. Under such circumstances, the intellectual debate between the "normal country" and "civilian power" visions would at last become linked to party competition. And if the crisis revealed an acute security vulnerability, the "autonomous great power" view could become ascendant, while the "pacifist state" perspective could wither away.

Much depends on the balance of power and the balance of commitment between the United States and China. If China's power and influence grew enormously, while U.S. power or commitment in East Asia declined proportionally, then Japan could "bandwagon" with China, rather than "balance" against China by adopting an accommodationist line similar to the "civilian power" concept.

Third, most of the influential conservative politicians who managed the normalization of relations with China have passed from the scene. As a result, political leaders are now more likely to view China soberly and make policy decisions based on calculations of national interest rather than feelings of guilt or romanticism.

Fourth, as the political ranks are increasingly dominated by those born after World War II, politicians of all parties will press for greater diplomatic autonomy from the United States and a bilateral alliance on more equal terms. They will, of course, disagree about the concrete content of this autonomy and equality, but that is a matter of tactics, not strategy.

Fifth, while the "political space" in which stridently pacifist politicians can operate has shrunk with the demise of the JSP, the space for nationalist politicians is likely to expand. In the era of one-party dominance, the nationalist right was subsumed and tamed within the LDP. With the split in the conservative camp, the voice of hard-core nationalists may become louder in the LDP, and the New Frontier Party could serve as an alternative outlet for their views. Although its direct impact on policymaking is likely to remain limited, the nationalist right could become increasingly unruly. It could complicate Japanese diplomacy by making more frequent statements about its interpretation of history and being more assertive about Japan's disputed territorial claims.

Bureaucratic Politics

The nature of policymaking at the bureaucratic level suggests incremental change, rather than dramatic shifts, in Japanese security policy. The power of the Japanese prime minister over the administrative agencies is limited compared with that of the U.S. president (or even the chief executives in most of the major west European states), and the bureaucratic agencies primarily in charge of security policy prefer the incremental and consensual approach.

The following is a brief snapshot of the key state actors in security policy.

The Prime Minister

In the past, factionalism within the ruling LDP and the need to manage a pacifist and neutralist opposition in the Diet prevented the prime minister from exercising strong leadership in foreign policy. Factional politics are less decisive in selecting the prime minister, and the opposition parties are now less ideological about foreign affairs. Nevertheless, the need to maintain interparty coalitions and manage policy divisions within the ruling party or parties continues to constrain the prime minister from pushing dramatic policy change.

During the mid-1980s, then–Prime Minister Nakasone tried to enhance his decisionmaking powers over the established ministries by creating foreign affairs and security policy offices within the prime minister's secretariat. The aim was to create something akin to the National Security Council staff in the United States. But this institutional innovation has yet to meet the objectives Nakasone had in mind.

Of course, much depends on the personality of the prime minister. With the dovish and weak Toshiki Kaifu as prime minister during the Persian Gulf crisis, the office of the prime minister exerted little leadership. By contrast, Hashimoto has been much more effective than his predecessor, Tomiichi Murayama, at defusing tensions in Okinawa in the wake of the rape incident. But it will remain difficult for even the best of prime ministers to achieve centralized executive coordination and leadership over the traditional ministries dominated by elite careerists.

The Ministry of Foreign Affairs (MOFA)

MOFA continues to be the agency that places the greatest priority on maintaining good relations with the United States. To some extent, MOFA is divided between its "Americanists" and "Asianists." For example, "Asianists" might be more receptive to Asian groupings, like the East Asian Economic Caucus, that exclude the United States. Another intra-MOFA subgroup is the so-called "China school," the diplomats with Chinese-language training and numerous postings in China-related jobs. Unlike the MOFA "Soviet school," which held hard-line views against the Soviet Union, the "China school" tends to favor accommodation to Chinese concerns.

Of late, MOFA has taken steps that have diminished the division between "Americanists" on the one hand and "Asianists" and the "China school" on the other. The creation of the General Foreign Policy Bureau (*Sogo Gaiko Seisaku Kyoku*) as a "super-bureau" has not only weakened the traditionally powerful North American Bureau, but also strengthened MOFA's ability to integrate the various strands of foreign policy. The appointment of a prominent "Americanist" as director-general of the Asia Bureau has helped minimize tensions between Japanese policy toward the United States and that toward Asia. For example, during the March 1996 Taiwan crisis, MOFA moved quickly to endorse the deployment of two U.S. carriers to the area. And now some MOFA "Asianists" see the wisdom of enhancing Japan's relations with East Asian states as a way of balancing Chinese influence. Nevertheless, the "China school" wants to avoid a deterioration in relations with China.

Japan Defense Agency (JDA)

In addition to managing the process of defense modernization, the JDA has traditionally stressed two missions: 1) strengthening public support for Japan's defense policy and the alliance with the United States, and 2) institutionalizing its control over the military. Although the JDA never managed to upgrade its status to a full-fledged ministry, and continues to have some of its top officials come from other ministries (like MOFA, the Ministry of Finance, the Ministry of International Trade and Industry, and the Police Agency), the agency's prestige has increased gradually, as indicated by the higher quality of its younger recruits. The JDA will cease to be a "colonized" agency as career JDA officials fill more and more of the agency's top posts.

Despite these trends, the end of the Cold War and the breakup of the LDP amounted to a setback for the JDA. JDA officials managed to revive some of their influence by cooperating closely with Pentagon officials to initiate a U.S.-Japan dialogue on security issues and by revising the National Defense Program Outline. But the limits of JDA influence became apparent when Prime Minister Hashimoto marginalized the agency in dealing with the Okinawa base issue.

The MOFA-JDA relationship

Despite sharing a strong commitment to the U.S.-Japan security relationship, MOFA and the JDA have long been bureaucratic rivals. MOFA's involvement in the details of defense policy derives primarily from having the U.S.-Japan Security Treaty Division (Ampo-ka), which is housed in MOFA's North American Bureau. The MOFA-JDA competition was especially intense during the Persian Gulf crisis, when some MOFA officials entertained a proposal to create an "international peace cooperation" unit separate from the Self-Defense Forces. The MOFA reorganization that placed U.N. policy within the General Foreign Policy Bureau is likely to perpetuate this bureaucratic rivalry.

Rivalry notwithstanding, both MOFA and JDA embrace an incrementalist approach to expanding Japan's security role and promoting defense cooperation with the United States. On the whole, MOFA officials do not want to complicate policymaking by provoking a constitutional debate, and they do not want to aggravate concerns in Asia by moving too quickly. JDA officials want to avoid jeopardizing the delicate public consensus on defense policy that they worked so diligently to nurture.

Ministry of Finance (MOF)

Despite the recent campaign to reform and even break up the Ministry of Finance, this fiscally conservative ministry will wield strong influence to restrain defense-related expenditures, and MOF will work with like-minded politicians to achieve its goals. At a time when Japan is again experiencing sizable budget deficits, and faces huge health and pension outlays for an aging population, the MOF may demand hard choices among different defense funding requirements—e.g., host-nation support versus the cost of relocating Okinawa bases versus funds for theater missile defense.

Ministry of International Trade and Industry (MITI)

MITI will continue to play an influential role in managing relations with the United States on issues of military technology. Although it might gingerly seek to relax restrictions on arms exports, it will also strive to protect the technological interests of Japanese firms.

MITI will work energetically to sustain the current nuclear energy policy of plutonium recycling.

Ministry of Transportation and Ministry of Posts and Telecommunications
These two ministries will impede JDA efforts to strengthen defense cooperation with the United States at the operational level during crises, especially for the use of civilian facilities.

Cabinet Legal Affairs Bureau
This bureau will insist on maintaining a restrictive interpretation of the constitution, especially regarding the use of force and the exercise of the collective self-defense right.

The above complex of bureaucratic interests makes it highly unlikely that there will be more than an incremental evolution in Japanese security policy without a major shift in the international environment, a structural realignment of party politics, or a serious domestic economic crisis. The limits on the prime minister's power also constrain the chief executive from pushing more dramatic change and could even hamper his ability to respond effectively to international crises.

CONCLUSION

The current dynamics of domestic politics suggest that Japan will make incremental changes to strengthen the alliance with the United States along the following lines:

• Revision of the U.S.-Japan Defense Cooperation Guidelines and the eventual passage of enabling legislation so that Japan can provide logistical support to U.S. forces in regional contingencies within the constraints of the current interpretation of the constitution;

• Cooperation with the United States to reduce some of the bases in Okinawa by creating new facilities (e.g., to compensate for the

[51]

return of the Futenma Marine Corps Air Station) and transferring some of the functions to other areas, but not altering significantly the level and character of the U.S. military presence in Japan;

• Modest enhancement of JSDF capabilities while implementing the force restructuring mandated by the new National Defense Program Outline, but no procurement of systems that can be construed as giving Japan a power projection capability (e.g., long-range transport capability and an aircraft carrier);

• Some support for joint R&D on theater missile defense, but little or no movement on acquisition and deployment.

Japan will also continue to promote the APEC process by modestly pushing economic liberalization while remaining sensitive to Asian concerns about development. Efforts will be made to maintain cordial relations with both South Korea and China, but no decisive steps will be taken that successfully convince Koreans and Chinese that Japan has sincerely dealt with its militarist past. Therefore, the concerns these countries express about Japanese remilitarization will feed back into the Japanese polity and obstruct a policy of expanding Japan's security role beyond the defense of the home islands. Japan will continue to cultivate the ASEAN Regional Forum as a multilateral security forum and perhaps move forward on a comparable dialogue for Northeast Asia.

The advantage of this incremental approach is that it builds on rather than upsets the domestic consensus that has emerged over the years in favor of the security alliance with the United States. It also reassures the rest of East Asia that Japan will not evolve into a great military power. But the danger of incrementalism is that these adjustments in the U.S.-Japan security relationship might not be enough to meet American expectations and that Japan might not be able to respond effectively to a regional security crisis (e.g., in Korea or over Taiwan). It might also prevent Japan from doing more to help prevent a regional security crisis from emerging.

— Grobal hegemony .. leader US. of Grobal village.
   still big gap, too early to think
   50 years later might be possible

→ but in near future,

MEMBERS OF THE
STUDY GROUP ON THE U.S.-JAPAN
SECURITY ALLIANCE

RICHARD LEE ARMITAGE, Study Group Co-Chair, is President of the Armitage Associates, L.C. From 1983 to 1989, he served as Assistant Secretary of Defense for International Security Affairs.

HAROLD BROWN, Study Group Co-Chair, has been a Counselor at the Center for Strategic and International Studies since July 1992. He was Secretary of Defense from 1977 to 1981.

BRUCE STOKES, Project Director, directs the Council's programs on international trade.

JAMES AUER, Vanderbilt University
SUSUMU AWANOHARA, Nikko Research Center, Inc.
DANIEL E. BOB, Office of Senator William V. Roth, U.S. Senate
JASON BRUZDZINSKI, Committee of National Security, U.S. House of Representatives
KENT E. CALDER, Princeton University
STEVE C. CLEMONS, Office of Senator Jeff Bingaman, U.S. Senate
PATRICK CRONIN, Institute for National Strategic Studies
GERALD L. CURTIS, Columbia University
JAMES DELANEY, Institute for Defense Analyses
DAVID B. H. DENOON, New York University
PETER ENNIS, *The Oriental Economist*
CARL FORD, Ford & Associates
YOICHI FUNABASHI, *Asahi Shimbun*
ROBERT L. GALLUCCI, Georgetown University
MICHAEL J. GREEN, Institute for Defense Analyses
DENNIS HEJLIK, Council on Foreign Relations
MARIUS B. JANSEN, Princeton University
ARNOLD KANTER, Forum for International Policy
RICHARD KESSLER, Office of Representative Howard L. Berman, U.S. House of Representatives

The U.S.-Japan Security Alliance in the 21st Century

HIROTSUGU KOIKE, *Nihon Keizai Shimbun*
YOSHIHISA KOMORI, *Sankei Shimbun*
ROBERT MANNING, Progressive Policy Institute
MIKE M. MOCHIZUKI, The Brookings Institution
DOUGLAS PAAL, Asia Pacific Policy Center
TORKEL PATTERSON, Pacific Forum CSIS
MICHAEL K. POWELL, U.S. Department of Justice
JAMES PRZYSTUP, Heritage Foundation
RICHARD J. SAMUELS, Massachusetts Institute of Technology
GARY SHIFFMAN, Office of Senator Connie Mack, U.S. Senate
JAMES SHINN, Council on Foreign Relations
SHEILA A. SMITH, Boston University
ALAN TONELSON, USBIC
PAUL D. WOLFOWITZ, School of Advanced International Studies,
    Johns Hopkins University
DONALD S. ZAGORIA, Hunter College

Note: Members participated as individuals and not in their institutional capacity. Affiliation is listed for information purposes only.

[54]

Completion of the Review of the Guidelines for U.S.-Japan Defense Cooperation

U.S.-Japan Security Consultative Committee

New York, New York

September 23, 1997

The U.S.-Japan alliance is indispensable for ensuring the security of Japan and continues to play a key role in maintaining peace and stability in the Asia-Pacific region. It also facilitates the positive engagement of the United States in the region. The alliance reflects such common values as respect for freedom, democracy, and human rights, and serves as a political basis for wide-ranging bilateral cooperation, including efforts to build a more stable international security environment. The success of such efforts benefits all in the region.

The "Guidelines for U.S.-Japan Defense Cooperation" (the Guidelines), approved by the 17th Security Consultative Committee (SCC) on November 27, 1978, resulted from studies and consultations on a comprehensive framework for cooperation in the area of defense. Significant achievements for closer defense cooperation under the Guidelines have increased the credibility of bilateral security arrangements.

Although the Cold War has ended, the potential for instability and uncertainty persists in the Asia-Pacific region. Accordingly, the maintenance of peace and stability in this region has assumed greater importance for the security of Japan.

The "U.S.-Japan Joint Declaration on Security," issued by President Clinton and Prime Minister Hashimoto in April 1996, reconfirmed that the U.S.-Japan security relationship remains the cornerstone for achieving common security objectives, and for maintaining a stable and prosperous environment in the Asia-Pacific region as we enter the 21st century. The President and the Prime Minister agreed to initiate a review of the 1978 Guidelines to build upon the close working relationship already established between the United States and Japan.

In June 1996, the two Governments reconstituted the Subcommittee for Defense Cooperation (SDC) under the auspices of the SCC, to conduct the review of the Guidelines (the Review) on the basis of Japan's "National Defense Program Outline" of November 1995, and the "U.S.–Japan Joint Declaration on Security." In view of the changes in the post–Cold War environment, and on the basis of the achievements made under the Guidelines, the SDC has considered:

- Cooperation under normal circumstances;
- Actions in response to an armed attack against Japan; and
- Cooperation in situations in areas surrounding Japan that will have an important influence on Japan's peace and security (situations in areas surrounding Japan).

These considerations aimed at providing a general framework and policy direction for the roles and missions of the two countries and ways of cooperation and coordination, both under normal circumstances and during contingencies. The Review did not address situations in specific areas.

The SDC has conducted the Review with the objective of identifying ideas and specific items that would contribute to more effective bilateral cooperation with the intention to complete the Review by autumn of 1997, as instructed by the SCC in September 1996. The discussions of the SDC in the course of the Review are summarized in the "Progress Report on the Guidelines Review for U.S.-Japan Defense Cooperation" of September 1996, and in the "Interim Report on the Review of the Guidelines for U.S.-Japan Defense Cooperation" of June 1997.

The SDC prepared and submitted to the SCC new "Guidelines for U.S.-Japan Defense Cooperation." The SCC approved and issued the following Guidelines, which supersede the 1978 Guidelines.

THE GUIDELINES FOR U.S.-JAPAN DEFENSE COOPERATION

I. THE AIM OF THE GUIDELINES

The aim of these Guidelines is to create a solid basis for more effective and credible U.S.-Japan cooperation under normal circumstances, in case of an armed attack against Japan, and in situations in areas surrounding Japan. The Guidelines also provide a general framework and policy direction for the roles and missions of the two countries and ways of cooperation and coordination, both under normal circumstances and during contingencies.

II. BASIC PREMISES AND PRINCIPLES

The Guidelines and programs under the Guidelines are consistent with the following basic premises and principles.
1. The rights and obligations under the Treaty of Mutual Cooperation and Security between the United States of America and Japan (the U.S.-Japan Security Treaty) and its related arrangements, as well as the fundamental framework of the U.S.-Japan alliance, will remain unchanged.
2. Japan will conduct all its actions within the limitations of its Constitution and in accordance with such basic positions as the maintenance of its exclusively defense-oriented policy and its three non-nuclear principles.
3. All actions taken by the United States and Japan will be consistent with basic principles of international law, including the peaceful settlement of disputes and sovereign equality, and relevant international agreements such as the Charter of the United Nations.
4. The Guidelines and programs under the Guidelines will not obligate either Government to take legislative, budgetary or administrative measures. However, since the objective of the Guidelines and programs under the Guidelines is to establish an effective framework for bilateral cooperation, the two

[57]

Governments are expected to reflect in an appropriate way the results of these efforts, based on their own judgments, in their specific policies and measures. All actions taken by Japan will be consistent with its laws and regulations then in effect.

III. COOPERATION UNDER NORMAL CIRCUMSTANCES

Both Governments will firmly maintain existing U.S.-Japan security arrangements. Each Government will make efforts to maintain required defense postures. Japan will possess defense capability within the scope necessary for self-defense on the basis of the "National Defense Program Outline." In order to meet its commitments, the United States will maintain its nuclear deterrent capability, its forward deployed forces in the Asia-Pacific region, and other forces capable of reinforcing those forward deployed forces.

Both Governments, based on their respective policies, under normal circumstances will maintain close cooperation for the defense of Japan as well as for the creation of a more stable international security environment.

Both Governments will under normal circumstances enhance cooperation in a variety of areas. Examples include mutual support activities under the Agreement between the Government of Japan and the Government of the United States of America concerning Reciprocal Provision of Logistic Support, Supplies and Services between the Self-Defense Forces of Japan and the Armed Forces of the United States of America; the Mutual Defense Assistance Agreement between the United States of America and Japan; and their related arrangements.

1. Information Sharing and Policy Consultations
   Recognizing that accurate information and sound analysis are at the foundation of security, the two Governments will increase information and intelligence sharing and the exchange of views on international situations of mutual interest, especially in the Asia-Pacific region. They will also continue close consultations on defense policies and military postures.
   Such information sharing and policy consultations will be

conducted at as many levels as possible and on the broadest range of subjects. This will be accomplished by taking advantage of all available opportunities, such as SCC and Security Sub-Committee (SSC) meetings.

2. Various Types of Security Cooperation
Bilateral cooperation to promote regional and global activities in the field of security contributes to the creation of a more stable international security environment.

Recognizing the importance and significance of security dialogues and defense exchanges in the region, as well as international arms control and disarmament, the two Governments will promote such activities and cooperate as necessary.

When either or both Governments participate in United Nations peacekeeping operations or international humanitarian relief operations, the two sides will cooperate closely for mutual support as necessary. They will prepare procedures for cooperation in such areas as transportation, medical services, information sharing, and education and training.

When either or both Governments conduct emergency relief operations in response to requests from governments concerned or international organizations in the wake of large-scale disasters, they will cooperate closely with each other as necessary.

3. Bilateral Programs
Both Governments will conduct bilateral work, including bilateral defense planning in case of an armed attack against Japan, and mutual cooperation planning in situations in areas surrounding Japan. Such efforts will be made in a comprehensive mechanism involving relevant agencies of the respective Governments, and establish the foundation for bilateral cooperation.

Bilateral exercises and training will be enhanced in order not only to validate such bilateral work but also to enable smooth and effective responses by public and private entities of both countries, starting with U.S. Forces and the Self-Defense Forces. The two Governments will under normal circumstances establish a bilateral coordination mechanism involving relevant agencies to be operated during contingencies.

IV. ACTIONS IN RESPONSE TO AN ARMED ATTACK AGAINST JAPAN

Bilateral actions in response to an armed attack against Japan remain a core aspect of U.S.-Japan defense cooperation.

When an armed attack against Japan is imminent, the two Governments will take steps to prevent further deterioration of the situation and make preparations necessary for the defense of Japan. When an armed attack against Japan takes place, the two Governments will conduct appropriate bilateral actions to repel it at the earliest possible stage.

1. When an Armed Attack against Japan Is Imminent
The two Governments will intensify information and intelligence sharing and policy consultations and initiate at an early stage the operation of a bilateral coordination mechanism. Cooperating as appropriate, they will make preparations necessary for ensuring coordinated responses according to the readiness stage selected by mutual agreement. Japan will establish and maintain the basis for U.S. reinforcements. As circumstances change, the two Governments will also increase intelligence gathering and surveillance, and will prepare to respond to activities which could develop into an armed attack against Japan.

The two Governments will make every effort, including diplomatic efforts, to prevent further deterioration of the situation.

Recognizing that a situation in areas surrounding Japan may develop into an armed attack against Japan, the two Governments will be mindful of the close interrelationship of the two requirements: preparations for the defense of Japan and responses to or preparations for situations in areas surrounding Japan.

2. When an Armed Attack against Japan Takes Place
(1) Principles for Coordinated Bilateral Actions
(a)   Japan will have primary responsibility immedi-

ately to take action and to repel an armed attack against Japan as soon as possible. The United States will provide appropriate support to Japan. Such bilateral cooperation may vary according to the scale, type, phase, and other factors of the armed attack. This cooperation may include preparations for and execution of coordinated bilateral operations, steps to prevent further deterioration of the situation, surveillance, and intelligence sharing

(b) In conducting bilateral operations, U.S. Forces and the Self-Defense Forces will employ their respective defense capabilities in a coordinated, timely, and effective manner. In doing this, they will conduct effective joint operations of their respective Forces' ground, maritime and air services. The Self-Defense Forces will primarily conduct defensive operations in Japanese territory and its surrounding waters and airspace, while U.S. Forces support Self-Defense Forces' operations. U.S. Forces will also conduct operations to supplement the capabilities of the Self-Defense Forces.

(c) The United States will introduce reinforcements in a timely manner, and Japan will establish and maintain the basis to facilitate these deployments.

(2) Concept of Operations
  (a) Operations to Counter Air Attack against Japan
    U.S. Forces and the Self-Defense Forces will bilaterally conduct operations to counter air attack against Japan.
    The Self-Defense Forces will have primary responsibility for conducting operations for air defense.
    U.S. Forces will support Self-Defense Forces' operations and conduct operations, including those

which may involve the use of strike power, to supplement the capabilities of the Self-Defense Forces.

(b) Operations to Defend Surrounding Waters and to Protect Sea Lines of Communication

U.S. Forces and the Self-Defense Forces will bilaterally conduct operations for the defense of surrounding waters and for the protection of sea lines of communication.

The Self-Defense Forces will have primary responsibility for the protection of major ports and straits in Japan, for the protection of ships in surrounding waters, and for other operations.

U.S. Forces will support Self-Defense Forces' operations and conduct operations, including those which may provide additional mobility and strike power, to supplement the capabilities of the Self-Defense Forces.

(c) Operations to Counter Airborne and Seaborne Invasions of Japan

U.S. Forces and the Self-Defense Forces will bilaterally conduct operations to counter airborne and seaborne invasions of Japan.

The Self-Defense Forces will have primary responsibility for conducting operations to check and repel such invasions.

U.S. Forces will primarily conduct operations to supplement the capabilities of the Self-Defense Forces. The United States will introduce reinforcements at the earliest possible stage, according to the scale, type, and other factors of the invasion, and will support Self-Defense Forces' operations.

(d) Responses to Other Threats

(i) The Self-Defense Forces will have primary responsibility to check and repel guerrilla-commando type attacks or any other unconventional attacks involving military infiltration in Japanese territory at the earliest possible stage. They will cooperate and coordinate closely with relevant agencies, and will be supported in appropriate ways by U.S. Forces depending on the situation.

(ii) U.S. Forces and the Self-Defense Forces will cooperate and coordinate closely to respond to a ballistic missile attack. U.S. Forces will provide Japan with necessary intelligence, and consider, as necessary, the use of forces providing additional strike power.

(3) Activities and Requirements for Operations
    (a) Command and Coordination

U.S. Forces and the Self-Defense Forces, in close cooperation, will take action through their respective command-and-control channels. To conduct effective bilateral operations, the two Forces will establish, in advance, procedures which include those to determine the division of roles and missions and to synchronize their operations.

    (b) Bilateral Coordination Mechanism

Necessary coordination among the relevant agencies of the two Governments will be conducted through a bilateral coordination mechanism. In order to conduct effective bilateral operations, U.S. Forces and the Self-Defense Forces will closely coordinate operations, intelligence activities, and logistics support through this coordination mechanism including use of a bilateral coordination center.

(c)   Communication/Electronics
    The two Governments will provide mutual support to ensure effective use of communications and electronics capabilities.

(d)   Intelligence Activities
    The two Governments will cooperate in intelligence activities in order to ensure effective bilateral operations. This will include coordination of requirements, collection, production, and dissemination of intelligence products. Each Government will be responsible for the security of shared intelligence.

(e)   Logistics Support Activities
    U.S. Forces and the Self-Defense Forces will conduct logistics support activities efficiently and properly in accordance with appropriate bilateral arrangements.
    To improve the effectiveness of logistics and to alleviate functional shortfalls, the two Governments will undertake mutual support activities, making appropriate use of authorities and assets of central and local government agencies, as well as private sector assets. Particular attention will be paid to the following points in conducting such activities:

(i) Supply
    The United States will support the acquisition of supplies for systems of U.S. origin while Japan will support the acquisition of supplies in Japan.

(ii)   Transportation
    The two Governments will closely cooperate in transportation operations, including airlift and sealift of supplies from the United States to Japan.

(iii) Maintenance

Japan will support the maintenance of U.S. Forces' equipment in Japan; the United States will support the maintenance of items of U.S. origin which are beyond Japanese maintenance capabilities. Maintenance support will include the technical training of maintenance personnel as required. Japan will also support U.S. Forces' requirement for salvage and recovery.

(iv) Facilities

Japan will, in case of need, provide additional facilities and areas in accordance with the U.S.-Japan Security Treaty and its related arrangements. If necessary for effective and efficient operations, U.S. Forces and the Self-Defense Forces will make bilateral use of Self-Defense Forces facilities and U.S. facilities and areas in accordance with the Treaty and its related arrangements.

(v) Medical Services

The two Governments will support each other in the area of medical services such as medical treatment and transportation of casualties.

V. COOPERATION IN SITUATIONS IN AREAS SURROUNDING JAPAN THAT WILL HAVE AN IMPORTANT INFLUENCE ON JAPAN'S PEACE AND SECURITY (SITUATIONS IN AREAS SURROUNDING JAPAN)

Situations in areas surrounding Japan will have an important influence on Japan's peace and security. The concept, situations in areas surrounding Japan, is not geographical but situational. The two Governments will make every effort, including diplomatic measures, to prevent such situations from occurring. When the two Governments reach a common assessment of the state of each situation, they will effectively coordinate their activities. In responding to such situations, measures taken may differ depending on circumstances.

1. When a Situation in Areas Surrounding Japan Is Anticipated

    When a situation in areas surrounding Japan is antici-
pated, the two Governments will intensify information and
intelligence sharing and policy consultations, including efforts
to reach a common assessment of the situation.

    At the same time, they will make every effort, including diplo-
matic efforts, to prevent further deterioration of the situation,
while initiating at an early stage the operation of a bilateral coordination mechanism, including use of a bilateral coordination
center. Cooperating as appropriate, they will make preparations necessary for ensuring coordinated responses according
to the readiness stage selected by mutual agreement. As circumstances change, they will also increase intelligence gathering and surveillance, and enhance their readiness to respond
to the circumstances.

2. Responses to Situations in Areas Surrounding Japan

    The two Governments will take appropriate measures, to
include preventing further deterioration of situations, in
response to situations in areas surrounding Japan. This will be
done in accordance with the basic premises and principles listed in Section II above and based on their respective decisions.
They will support each other as necessary in accordance with
appropriate arrangements.

    Functions and fields of cooperation and examples of items
of cooperation are outlined below, and listed in the Annex.

3. Cooperation in Activities Initiated by Either Government

    Although either Government may conduct the following
activities at its own discretion, bilateral cooperation will
enhance their effectiveness.

    (a)   Relief Activities and Measures to Deal with Refugees
           Each Government will conduct relief activities
           with the consent and cooperation of the authorities
           in the affected area. The two Governments will coop-

erate as necessary, taking into account their respective capabilities.

The two Governments will cooperate in dealing with refugees as necessary. When there is a flow of refugees into Japanese territory, Japan will decide how to respond and will have primary responsibility for dealing with the flow; the United States will provide appropriate support.

(b)   Search and Rescue

The two Governments will cooperate in search and rescue operations. Japan will conduct search and rescue operations in Japanese territory; and at sea around Japan, as distinguished from areas where combat operations are being conducted. When U.S. Forces are conducting operations, the United States will conduct search and rescue operations in and near the operational areas.

(c)   Noncombatant Evacuation Operations

When the need arises for U.S. and Japanese noncombatants to be evacuated from a third country to a safe haven, each Government is responsible for evacuating its own nationals as well as for dealing with the authorities of the affected area. Instances in which each decides it is appropriate, the two Governments will coordinate in planning and cooperate in carrying out their evacuations, including for the securing of transportation means, transportation and the use of facilities, using their respective capabilities in a mutually supplementary manner. If similar need arises for noncombatants other than of U.S. or Japanese nationality, the respective countries may consider extending, on their respective terms, evacuation assistance to third country nationals.

(d) Activities for Ensuring the Effectiveness of Economic Sanctions for the Maintenance of International Peace and Stability

Each Government will contribute to activities for ensuring the effectiveness of economic sanctions for the maintenance of international peace and stability. Such contributions will be made in accordance with each Government's own criteria.

Additionally, the two Governments will cooperate with each other as appropriate, taking into account their respective capabilities. Such cooperation includes information sharing, and cooperation in inspection of ships based on United Nations Security Council Resolutions.

(2) Japan's Support for U.S. Forces Activities

(a) Use of Facilities

Based on the U.S.-Japan Security Treaty and its related arrangements, Japan will, in case of need, provide additional facilities and areas in a timely and appropriate manner, and ensure the temporary use by U.S. Forces of Self-Defense Forces facilities and civilian airports and ports.

(b) Rear Area Support

Japan will provide rear area support to those U.S. Forces that are conducting operations for the purpose of achieving the objectives of the U.S.-Japan Security Treaty. The primary aim of this rear area support is to enable U.S. Forces to use facilities and conduct operations in an effective manner. By its very nature, Japan's rear area support will be provided primarily in Japanese territory. It may also be provided on the high seas and in international airspace around Japan which are distinguished from areas where combat operations are being conducted.

In providing rear area support, Japan will make appropriate use of authorities and assets of the central and local government agencies, as well as private sector assets. The Self-Defense Forces, as appropriate, will provide such support consistent with their mission for the defense of Japan and the maintenance of public order.

(3)   U.S.-Japan Operational Cooperation

As situations in areas surrounding Japan have an important influence on Japan's peace and security, the Self-Defense Forces will conduct such activities as intelligence gathering, surveillance and minesweeping, to protect lives and property and to ensure navigational safety. U.S. Forces will conduct operations to restore the peace and security affected by situations in areas surrounding Japan.

With the involvement of relevant agencies, cooperation and coordination will significantly enhance the effectiveness of both forces' activities.

VI.   BILATERAL PROGRAMS FOR EFFECTIVE DEFENSE COOPERATION UNDER THE GUIDELINES

Effective bilateral defense cooperation under the Guidelines will require the United States and Japan to conduct consultative dialogue throughout the spectrum of security conditions: normal circumstances, an armed attack against Japan, and situations in areas surrounding Japan. Both sides must be well informed and coordinate at multiple levels to ensure successful bilateral defense cooperation. To accomplish this, the two Governments will strengthen their information and intelligence sharing and policy consultations by taking advantage of all available opportunities, including SCC and SSC meetings, and they will establish the following two mechanisms to facilitate consultations, coordinate policies, and coordinate operational functions.

First, the two Governments will develop a comprehensive mechanism for bilateral planning and the establishment of common standards and procedures, involving not only U.S. Forces and the

Self-Defense Forces but also other relevant agencies of their respective Governments.

The two Governments will, as necessary, improve this comprehensive mechanism. The SCC will continue to play an important role for presenting policy direction to the work to be conducted by this mechanism. The SCC will be responsible for presenting directions, validating the progress of work, and issuing directives as necessary. The SDC will assist the SCC in bilateral work.

Second, the two Governments will also establish, under normal circumstances, a bilateral coordination mechanism that will include relevant agencies of the two countries for coordinating respective activities during contingencies.

1. Bilateral Work for Planning and Establishment of Common Standards and Procedures

    Bilateral work listed below will be conducted in a comprehensive mechanism involving relevant agencies of the respective Governments in a deliberate and efficient manner. Progress and results of such work will be reported at significant milestones to the SCC and the SDC.

    (1) Bilateral Defense Planning and Mutual Cooperation Planning

    U.S. Forces and the Self-Defense Forces will conduct bilateral defense planning under normal circumstances to take coordinated actions smoothly and effectively in case of an armed attack against Japan. The two Governments will conduct mutual cooperation planning under normal circumstances to be able to respond smoothly and effectively to situations in areas surrounding Japan.

    Bilateral defense planning and mutual cooperation planning will assume various possible situations, with the expectation that results of these efforts will be appropriately reflected in the plans of the two Governments. The two Governments will coordinate and adjust their plans in light of actual circumstances. The two Governments will be mindful that bilateral defense planning and mutual cooperation planning must be consistent so that appropriate responses will be ensured when a situation in areas surrounding Japan threatens to develop into an armed attack against Japan or when such a situation and an armed attack against Japan occur simultaneously.

(2) Establishment of Common Standards for Preparations

The two Governments will establish under normal circumstances common standards for preparations for the defense of Japan. These standards will address such matters as intelligence activities, unit activities, movements and logistics support in each readiness stage. When an armed attack against Japan is imminent, both Governments will agree to select a common readiness stage that will be reflected in the level of preparations for the defense of Japan by U.S. Forces, the Self-Defense Forces and other relevant agencies.

The two Governments will similarly establish common standards for preparations of cooperative measures in situations in areas surrounding Japan so that they may select a common readiness stage by mutual agreement.

(3) Establishment of Common Procedures

The two Governments will prepare in advance common procedures to ensure smooth and effective execution of coordinated U.S. Forces and Self-Defense Forces operations for the defense of Japan. These will include procedures for communications, transmission of target information, intelligence activities and logistics support, and prevention of fratricide. Common procedures will also include criteria for properly controlling respective unit operations. The two forces

will take into account the importance of communi-
cations/electronics interoperability, and will determine in advance their mutual requirements.

2. Bilateral Coordination Mechanism
    The two Governments will establish under normal cir-
cumstances a bilateral coordination mechanism involving relevant agencies of the two countries to coordinate respective
activities in case of an armed attack against Japan and in situations in areas surrounding Japan.
    Procedures for coordination will vary depending upon
items to be coordinated and agencies to be involved. They may
include coordination committee meetings, mutual dispatch of
liaison officers, and designation of points of contacts. As part
of such a bilateral coordination mechanism, U.S. Forces and
the Self-Defense Forces will prepare under normal circumstances
a bilateral coordination center with the necessary hardware and
software in order to coordinate their respective activities.

VII. TIMELY AND APPROPRIATE REVIEW OF THE GUIDELINES
The two Governments will review the Guidelines in a timely and
appropriate manner when changes in situations relevant to the
U.S.-Japan security relationship occur and if deemed necessary in
view of the circumstances at that time.

Workshop on the U.S.-Japan Guidelines for Defense Cooperation and the Future of Asian Security

On September 23, 1997, the United States and Japan issued newly revised Guidelines for Defense Cooperation. The new Guidelines identified areas for joint bilateral action in peacetime, in the defense of Japan against direct attack, and in response to regional crises. On September 29, 1997, the Council on Foreign Relations held a half-day seminar on the Guidelines with U.S. and Japanese government officials and security experts from the region to put the Guidelines in proper strategic perspective and enhance regional transparency on defense policy. The meeting was sponsored by the U.S.-Japan Foundation.

The seminar opened with comments by Paula Dobriansky, director of the Washington Program of the Council, and U.S.-Japan Foundation President Julia Chang Bloch. Michael Green, Olin Fellow for National Security Studies, then chaired a round-table of experts from the region, including: Dr. Kil Jeong-Woo, a former Republic of Korea (ROK) foreign ministry official now with the *Joong—Ahn Daily News*; Dr. Wang Jianwei, an assistant professor at the University of Wisconsin at Stevens Point who has published extensively on the People's Republic of China's (PRC) views of security; Dr. Anna Shkuropat, dean of International Studies at Vladivostok State University and an adviser to the Russian government on Asia-Pacific Affairs; and Dr. Kazuya Sakamoto, a diplomatic historian and expert on diplomatic history at Osaka University.[1] Following the roundtable, presentations were made by two of the key government officials behind the Guidelines review: Dr. Kurt Campbell, deputy assistant secretary of defense for Asia-Pacific affairs,

---

[1] It should be noted that these experts did not speak as official representatives of their governments.

and Mr. Ichiro Fujisaki, political minister at the Embassy for Japan in Washington, D.C. A summary of their remarks follows.

THE U.S. VIEW
Michael J. Green, Council on Foreign Relations

The key word that U.S. Secretary of State Madeleine Albright and Secretary of Defense William Cohen used last week to describe the Guidelines was "stability." To the extent that the United States and Japan have eliminated some of the uncertainty about where the alliance is heading, that characterization is true.

The April 1996 Joint Security Declaration, signed during President Clinton's visit to Japan, enhanced the political credibility of the alliance. However, a military alliance also needs operational credibility. At the operational level, the U.S.-Japan alliance was never really invoked during the Cold War. Only afterwards, during the 1990–91 Gulf War and the 1994 Korean Nuclear Crisis, was the U.S.-Japan alliance really tested. Arguably, the alliance failed both those tests, raising serious questions about its future. Hence the Guidelines review, which was intended to infuse the alliance with the operational credibility it lacked.

We have to refer to the 1978 Guidelines to understand the contemporary perspective on Tokyo's role in regional crises in the areas around Japan. The 1978 Guidelines covered bilateral planning in three contexts: normal circumstances; a direct attack on Japan; and crises in the Far East. While guidance for bilateral cooperation in the first two areas was detailed, in the third it was more vague, due to reluctance both in Tokyo and other regional capitals to define Japan's broader security role. The failure to outline bilateral cooperation in regional security was not an immediate problem because, in the context of the Cold War, Japan could play a significant but quiet political-military role without explicitly addressing its potential role in a regional crisis. In particular, Japan's proximity to the Soviet Union allowed Tokyo and Washington to use the threat of a direct attack on Japan to justify its contribution to the U.S. strategy of containment. However, with the end of the Cold War, the issue of Japan's contribution to regional security was once again left unresolved—

as was seen during the Gulf War and in the Korean nuclear crisis.

While preserving the basic framework of the U.S.-Japan alliance, the 1997 Guidelines filled in the gaps from the third part of the 1978 Guidelines. This was extremely important for the operational, and therefore political, credibility of the alliance. The 1997 revision addressed issues that should have been dealt with a long time ago.

However, there remain unresolved issues. One is the definition of the area around Japan and, in particular, whether Taiwan is included. In my own view, there was never really any answer other than the one that the two governments came up with, which was neither to explicitly include nor to explicitly exclude the island from the defense perimeter. Taiwan could not have been excluded, because the implication would be that the United States and Japan do not care what happens in the area around Taiwan. That, of course, is not true. On the other hand, if Taiwan had been included explicitly, China would be provoked unnecessarily, and Taiwan would be stimulated unnecessarily. This latter course also would have been inconsistent with the "one China policy" pursued by the United States and Japan.

Another issue is whether Japan can formally recognize the right to engage in collective defense. That is, in addition to working with the United States to protect Japanese security, can Japan use force to help the United States defend its forces in the Far East? The Guidelines have avoided the issue of collective defense. The notion that Japan has the right to collective defense under international law but not under Japanese political and constitutional law is not very convincing. Many people, particularly in Japan, would like to see Tokyo play a larger regional role. However, you will hear from the regional panel some compelling reasons why this was not the time to push for collective defense. Moreover, in Japanese domestic politics, the new Guidelines' popularity—a recent poll indicated 65 percent of the Japanese public support the Guidelines—is due to the Guidelines' having been revised within the comfortable framework of the existing constitution.

Washington and Tokyo now must weave the Guidelines part of the fabric of the U.S.-Japan relationship through legislation, deliberate military planning, and joint training. The Guidelines are big news, but are in fact only a first step. The real test will come in the implementation phase.

THE SOUTH KOREAN VIEW
Dr. Kil Jeong-Woo, Jong—Ang Daily News

My presentation deals with two issues: first, the view of the South Korean (ROK) government and public on the Guidelines; and second, the Guidelines' significance for a contingency on the Korean peninsula. I then conclude with Seoul's expectations of Washington and Tokyo with respect to the Guidelines.

The official South Korean view on the Guidelines is one of "support with caution." In principle, the South Korean government supports the Guidelines because they were shaped with the possibility of contingencies on the Korean peninsula as their immediate focal point. It is cautious, however, because the Guidelines may signal a reduction in the American presence in the region. This worries the Korean public: in recent years, surveys have consistently ranked the United States as the most reliable ally and Japan as the least reliable.

One can thus characterize the South Korean view as one of ambivalence, a feeling that is reinforced by South Korea's uncertainty with respect to both North Korea and the future of Sino-U.S. relations. South Koreans are supportive of the U.S. military presence on Okinawa, and therefore of the Guidelines, because they know the importance of U.S.-Japan security cooperation to Korea's own defense. However, they are also aware of China's displeasure with the new Guidelines, and fear that worsening relations between the two could undermine the region's long-term stability.

The Guidelines have not softened South Korea's aversion toward a strong Japanese role in any Korean conflict. The South Korean government has made it clear that under no circumstance can Japanese Self-Defense Forces intervene in Korean territorial waters or airspace, even in situations involving noncombatant emergency evacuation operations. Should evacuation of Japanese civilians be required, the South Korean government recommends the initial use of civilian Japanese aircraft or ships. If Japanese civilian ships are used to evacuate Japanese civilians, some kind of military ships will probably be used as escorts. South Korea does expect Japan to be involved in the evacuation of an estimated 200,000 to 300,000 refugees who would be uprooted in the initial months of fighting.

South Korea's longer-term view of the Guidelines will be shaped by their effect on relations between the three nations. First, Seoul expects the alliance's present level of transparency to continue. Second, most Koreans feel that as long as the U.S.-Japan security treaty and Japanese democracy are sustained, Japanese militarism will remain dormant. Third, in the strategic realm, there should be more substantive dialogue between Seoul and Tokyo. Fourth, the U.S.-ROK security alliance also should be discussed and redefined in preparation for the postunification era. Fifth, South Koreans expect the Japanese to think seriously about the "costs of peace" and to take a proactive posture in trilateral cooperation among Seoul, Washington, and Tokyo to engage North Korea. Finally, the Guidelines might be a good start toward turning Japan into a "normal country"—a reliable partner with courage to confront the dark side of its history.

THE CHINESE VIEW
Wang Jianwei, University of Wisconsin

China's attitude toward the U.S.-Japan Guidelines can be understood at both the macro and the micro levels. At the macro level, China, like Russia, has been very suspicious. Chinese President Jiang Zemin, in his report to the 15th Party Congress, articulated China's formal position on this issue for the first time, stating that strengthening military alliances is not conducive to world peace and stability. In China's opinion, these military alliances are "leftovers" from the Cold War and should be dismantled rather than expanded.

Accordingly, alliances should be replaced by new patterns of security cooperation. Like Russia, China has never been convinced by the various reasons offered by the United States for strengthening alliances in the post–Cold War period. For Beijing, the security environment in East Asia has been relatively calm and stable compared to Europe, and there is no need for Japan and the United States to expand military cooperation. Assuming that a military alliance needs a hypothetical enemy, Beijing remains unconvinced that the U.S.-Japan security alliance is needed in the present circumstances.

China sees a logical linkage between NATO expansion in Europe and the consolidation of the U.S.-Japan alliance in East Asia. According to this view, the larger strategic purpose for the United States is to perpetuate and institutionalize its strategic superiority as the sole global superpower. The enlargement of NATO and the revision of the U.S.-Japan alliance are designed to deprive Russia and China of geopolitical resources. Thus, China perceives the revitalization of the U.S.-Japan security alliance not as an isolated incident, but as part of a global U.S. strategy.

The timing of the U.S.-Japan decision to revise the Guidelines reinforces this Chinese perception. It was in the wake of the Taiwan Straits crisis that President Clinton and Prime Minister Hashimoto decided to revise the Guidelines to expand the scope of security cooperation to areas surrounding Japan. Even during the heyday of the Soviet threat, the 1978 Guidelines did not extend the scope of the alliance and dealt only with situations concerning an attack by the Soviet Union on Japan. So the Chinese ask the basic questions: Why now? Is today's "China threat" already bigger than the Soviet threat that existed in the 1970s and the 1980s?

At the micro level, I think China realizes that the American military presence in East Asia is a fact of life and it will remain so for a very long time. China also understands that the American troops in the region do serve certain stabilizing functions, although it would be a stretch to suggest, as some American officials have done, that China is the largest beneficiary of the U.S. military presence in the region. Because of the stabilizing function of the U.S. presence, China has never formally demanded the total withdrawal of U.S. forces in the region. The fact that China continues to allow the U.S. Navy to pay port calls to Hong Kong after the handover clearly indicates Beijing's view that the U.S. presence is a stabilizing influence in the region. In other words, China does not see the U.S. military presence in Asia as a normal phenomenon in the long run. But provided that U.S.-Japan security cooperation does not affect its perceived security interests adversely, China does not intend to challenge the status quo in the short run.

China is concerned more about Japan's long-term military role in the Asia-Pacific region than the role of the United States. This concern has a long historical background. As early as the late 1940s, China worried that the United States would one day "let the Japanese loose." The current circumstance is no exception. Chinese analysts declare that the redefinition of the U.S.-Japan relationship is not the continuation of an old alliance, but rather represents the formation of a new military alliance. The key to this new alliance is the role of Japan, with the United States allowing it to extend its military functions to the entire Asia-Pacific region. Consequently, Japan's role in U.S. military strategy has been transformed from that of a passive to an active participant. In Chinese eyes, this result is not caused solely by U.S. pressure, but also by Japan's desire to become a political-military power in the region. The Chinese doubt that the Japanese will be forever satisfied as a mere economic power, and expect that Japan will someday become a full-fledged military power. Indeed, to many Chinese, Japan is already a military power. Therefore, the Chinese view is that rather than accelerating Japan's military role, the United States should slow it down.

Chinese leaders suspect that the United States might like to boost the Japanese military role in the region largely because both Washington and Tokyo share certain common interests with respect to Taiwan. To Beijing, the United States and Japan do not want to see the reunification of the mainland and Taiwan; instead, they tend to view Taiwan as an unsinkable aircraft carrier that can be used to constrain China. Perhaps for historical reasons, Japan might even be eager to keep Taiwan away from China. While officials from the United States have been cautious about spelling out the geographical definition of the areas around Japan, Japanese officials have been more blunt, even saying that Taiwan is clearly included in the scope of U.S.-Japan security cooperation.

These are some of the Chinese perceptions on this issue at both the macro and micro levels. In the context of these Chinese views, how will China react to the final version of the U.S.-Japan Defense Cooperation Guidelines? My guess is that, in the long run, China's deep-rooted concerns will remain. However, in the short-term, Beijing might find that the Guidelines are the best deal it can get under the present circumstances. The Guidelines define the "areas around Japan" as "situational" rather than as a "geographic" concept, and while such a definition fails to explicitly exclude Taiwan from the sphere of U.S.-Japan security cooperation, it does not explicitly include Taiwan either. The Guidelines also reiterate that Japan will conduct all its actions within the limitations of the Peace Constitution and maintain its exclusively defense-oriented military policy. Furthermore, the Guidelines also point out that U.S.-Japan defense cooperation is not targeted at any third country.

I think that all such statements in the Guidelines will make Beijing less uncomfortable. That is why Beijing has not directly and publicly criticized the Guidelines. Foreign Minister Qian Qichen did not even want to comment on the Guidelines. It is unlikely that China will make the Guidelines a big issue in its bilateral relations with either Japan or the United States. Still, no matter how sensitive the United States and Japan are to Chinese feelings, strengthening the U.S.-Japan alliance is largely at odds with the American policy of engaging China. From the U.S. perspective, this paradox might be inevitable, a result of its own uncertainties about China's long-term global and regional foreign policy intentions and objectives.

Nevertheless, the negative impact of the U.S.-Japan Guidelines on U.S.-China and Japan-China relations can be minimized by taking certain constructive measures. First, it is important to increase the transparency of U.S.-Japan security cooperation. The new Guidelines made efforts in this direction by clearly identifying the situations under which the mutual cooperation would be invoked. In the same spirit, during the implementation of the Guidelines, maximum transparency should also be maintained. In this respect, the Japanese practice of sending senior officials to Beijing to explain the revised Guidelines is a useful channel to increase transparency. Although they do not say so publicly, Chinese officials greatly appreciate such gestures of sensitivity toward China's concerns.

Second, perhaps the most effective way to alleviate Chinese suspicions about the Guidelines is to maintain stable and healthy bilateral relations. The Chinese have made it very clear, as early as 1990, that their attitude toward the U.S.-Japan alliance depends largely on the state of Sino-U.S. relations. History tells us that if the Sino-U.S. relationship can be stabilized in a strategic framework, the Chinese will be much less concerned with the American military presence in Asia and with U.S.-Japan security cooperation. Thus Japanese Prime Minister Hashimoto did the right thing in his recent visit to China by seeking to improve Sino-Japanese relations in other areas such as economic cooperation, World Trade Organization (WTO) negotiations, and territorial disputes. For the United States, the most effective way to compensate for the possible negative impact of the Guidelines is to try to make a success of state visits, such as the October 1997 visit by President Jiang, and to establish a so-called "strategic partnership" with China.

Among the Asian countries and entities, Taiwan has reacted most positively toward the publication of the Guidelines. President Lee Tenghui boasted that the Guidelines were devised largely with an eye to Taiwan's increased political power and international status, as well as its emergence as a nation of freedom and democracy. This is exactly the type of language that the United States and Japan would like to publicly deny, and which Beijing worries about most. Together, the United States and Japan should send a clear signal to Taiwan that the new security Guidelines do not imply an endorsement of Taiwanese political independence.

The United States and Japan should intensify their security consultation with China, both in bilateral and multilateral terms. In the final analysis, the U.S.-Japan bilateral security alliance alone is not adequate to maintain peace and stability in East Asia. A multilateral security framework is needed. While not currently viable, this framework could begin with a regular trilateral security consultation among the major powers in the region—the United States, Japan, and China. Though China is often criticized as being too bilaterally oriented in its diplomacy, are the United States and Japan prepared to engage China in a regular trilateral security forum?

In conclusion, the revised Guidelines on East Asian security should be viewed not just through their impact on the U.S.-Japan relationship, but also from the dynamic interaction between the United States, Japan, and China. Without China's goodwill and understanding, a consolidated U.S.-Japan security treaty might divide rather than unite Asia. A repeat of the Cold War polarization of Asia, this time with China as the enemy, must be avoided.

THE RUSSIAN VIEW
Anna Shkuropat, Vladivostok State University

Russia's interests and policy in the Asia-Pacific region changed fundamentally in the 1990s. Moscow saw the 1978 Guidelines as a threat to Soviet sea lanes, to the Soviet submarine bastion in the Sea of Okhotsk, and to the Kremlin's diplomatic leverage in the region. Today, Russia does not have the same level of active naval forces in the region, and Moscow's main focus with respect to the Asia-Pacific region is economic rather than strategic.

In short, the Russian government has a positive view of the Guidelines. This equanimity can be perceived from a number of facts: the visit by Deputy Prime Minister Nemstov in August 1997; the Kremlin's endorsement of the November 1, 1997, Hashimoto-Yeltsin meeting; and the planned visit by Prime Minister Chernomyrdin after the Hashimoto-Yeltsin meeting.

While expecting transparency and consultation in their implementation, the Kremlin sees opportunities emerging from the U.S.-Japan Guidelines. First, the U.S.-Japan alliance contributes to regional security, providing some balance with respect to China and keeping Japan under U.S. leadership. Second, Russia sees an opportunity to prove its good intentions to Japan while also building a more productive bilateral economic relationship. Third, Russia sees the Guidelines as enhancing the stability on the Korean peninsula.

THE JAPANESE VIEW
Kazuya Sakamoto, Osaka University

Japan's view on the Guidelines can be summarized in terms of four "C's." The first "C" refers to "cooperation," in particular, defense cooperation. By strengthening U.S.-Japan defense cooperation, the Guidelines will enhance the credibility of both the alliance and Japan's Self-Defense forces. The second "C" is "consultation." The Guidelines should lead to greater consultation between the United States

Appendixes

and Japan on regional security issues. This will empower Japan to shape American responses to regional crises and should put an end to the current system of "prior consultation" in which U.S. forces in Japan are deployed without the Japanese government's full cognizance of their missions. The third "C" is "collective self-defense." The Guidelines have not resolved the issue of collective defense. Eventually, the relevance of the constitutional prohibition on the right of belligerency (as described in Article 9 of the Japanese constitution) will have to be addressed directly and comprehensively. The fourth "C" refers to China. Japan does not want to be accused of ganging up on China, but Tokyo also fears another "Nixon shock" in which U.S. overtures to Beijing come as a surprise.

THE OFFICIAL JAPANESE VIEW
Ichiro Fujisaki, Political Minister, Embassy of Japan

Why were the Guidelines reviewed? As some have pointed out earlier this morning, the last time the Guidelines were reviewed was in 1978, during the Cold War. After nineteen years, the Guidelines became obsolete, and both Washington and Tokyo thought that it was time to review them.

How are the present Guidelines different from the 1978 version? The main difference is that the 1997 Guidelines focus more on the areas surrounding Japan.

Let me elaborate on the three major principles used in drafting the Guidelines. The first principle is that the rights and obligations under the Treaty of Mutual Cooperation and Security and related arrangements between the United States and Japan will remain unchanged. This is very important. Dr. Wang Jianwei has said that there are some concerns in the region that the two governments are widening the scope of U.S.–Japan security arrangements. These concerns are unfounded for two reasons. First, this is a document of agreement between two governments, not a treaty that must be ratified by the Japanese Diet and the U.S. Senate. We cannot change the scope of the preexisting U.S.-Japan Security Treaty by virtue of the 1997 Guidelines. Second, it is the thinking and the will of the Japanese people not to change the scope of existing security arrangements.

The second principle is that Japan will conduct any military actions within the limitations of its constitution and maintain its "exclusively defense-oriented" security policies and three nonnuclear principles. There was some mention that Japan is not happy with its status as a mere economic power and might seek to become a military power. I was very happy to learn that Japan is still deemed to be an economic power. We will never again be a military power because this is not the wish of the Japanese people. We have clearly stated on every occasion that we will never again be a military power and we will not change that basic position.

The third principle is that all actions taken by the United States and Japan will be consistent with basic tenets of international law.

Let me also say that in the process of reviewing the Guidelines, we have tried to be very transparent and, indeed, will continue to be transparent. First, we issued an unprecedented interim report in June, realizing that people in the United States, Japan, and the region were very interested in what we were discussing. Second, we dispatched delegations of high-level officials to neighboring countries to explain the content of the interim report. Now, even as we speak, our officials are in some of the neighboring countries explaining the content of the final report.

As for relations with China, as Dr. Wang said, our prime minister has gone to Beijing to explain our position. I think that after this mission to explain the final report, we will receive more understanding. I am very happy that Dr. Wang has said that although the Chinese government will not publicly say so, in reality Beijing greatly appreciates the efforts made by the Japanese and U.S. governments.

Contingencies in areas surrounding Japan were a focus of discussion after the issuance of the interim report. We tried to stipulate in the final report that we cannot specify geographical surrounding areas or situations. As a next step, the United States and Japan will proceed and discuss joint operational planning sometime this fall.

Appendixes

THE OFFICIAL U.S. VIEW
Kurt Campbell, Deputy Assistant Secretary of
Defense for Asia-Pacific Affairs

I want to talk about two things: first, the motivations behind the review; and second, the steps that will come next.

To understand the motivations behind the review, one must think back to the situation of two to three years ago, both in terms of the state of U.S.-Japan relations and broader regional security. Three years ago, an attempt to renew the Guidelines would not have attracted much attention outside of government. The alliance had been taken for granted in the region. However, as the U.S. government digested three specific occurrences, it became clear that we faced, if not a crisis, then at least concerns about the credibility of the alliance. These occurrences catalyzed the Guidelines review.

First, the United States and Japan failed to achieve a coordinated response to the Persian Gulf War. Japan was very generous with its financial contribution, but actual substantive consultation between Japan and the United States proved to be inadequate.

Second, effective coordination was again lacking during the 1993–94 nuclear crisis on the Korean peninsula. Again, there was uncertainty about what the United States could expect from Japan in terms of rear area support in the event of some sort of contingency. There were also questions within Japan itself about what it could do to support the United States if such a crisis arose.

Less frequently mentioned in the press was a third, more subtle, reason for revising the Guidelines: flagging Japanese popular support for the security relationship. Beginning in 1992–93, a series of Japanese opinion polls indicated a precipitous decline in the proportion of Japanese citizens who saw the U.S.-Japan security partnership as healthy, and as a positive foundation for Asian-Pacific stability. At the same time, there was significant discussion, both in Tokyo and elsewhere, about Japan's other security options. There was discussion about whether Japan should rely more on a multilateral security framework, or even take on security challenges on its own. Others suggested that Japan should reach a rapprochement with China, with China being the bigger brother and Japan playing a lesser role.

In the dialogue leading to the new Guidelines, the U.S. and Japanese governments accepted as self-evident that the U.S.-Japan alliance should remain relevant well into the 21st century. Our belief was, and continues to be, that the U.S.-Japan alliance can transcend the Cold War and that successful alliances adapt to new circumstances, evolving in ways that are healthy for both countries. Therefore, as we began the Guidelines process, which involved issuing the security declaration in April last year, our focus exceeded the narrow issue of roles and missions. Instead, we aggressively sought to bring a new character to the alliance, and to enhance and increase the quality of our dialogue. Our belief was that, for the alliance to maintain its viability, its very nature would have to change in a number of ways: consultations would have to be more regular; the United States would have to treat Japan as an equal in how we think about policy issues and how we formulate our regional strategies; and, as a result, Japan would have to take on more responsibilities, both diplomatically and in terms of the Guidelines review process. Through this dialogue, we believe we have restored the credibility to the alliance that has underwritten stability in the Asia-Pacific region.

With respect to next steps, I would underscore Minister Fujisaki's point that rather than focusing simply on the content of the Guidelines, which are very important, we must think about the process as well. One of the interesting things about Asia-Pacific security matters is the almost complete lack of transparency of internal defense requirements, procurement goals, regional security ambitions, and, indeed, the scope and content of a whole variety of regional bilateral defense arrangements. What the defense Guidelines have done is to bring a level of transparency heretofore unseen in Asia-Pacific security matters. We issued a multipage review, free from secret agreements and private annexes. We issued an interim report as well, giving interested parties in the region and elsewhere a view into the alliance's evolution.

The Guidelines review will now go forward on many levels, and I want to talk about those levels very specifically. I will begin with transparency in the region. Just as there are U.S. and Japanese officials giving briefings throughout the region now, we must continue to inform the region as our work progresses. The transparency that has been part and parcel of this process is perhaps the most important contribution to East Asian stability as we go forward. With this in mind, we also think that it is important for others in the region to share their own initiatives. For instance, China and Russia have been involved in an extremely ambitious, multitiered process of security dialogue and confidence-building measures. I, for one, would like to be briefed on that and would like to know more from China and Russia about their ultimate goals. That kind of transparency should not simply be applied to the Guidelines review, but to all major strategic innovations in the region as a whole.

In addition to bilateral means of reassurances, there is also the subject of multilateral discussion. We will use the ASEAN Regional Forum as a locus for multilateral dialogue about the Guidelines review. In October 1997, the Japanese Self-Defense Agency will be hosting a session in Tokyo in which all from the region are invited to be briefed and to ask questions about the Guidelines. In addition to the broader multilateral opportunities for briefings on the Guidelines, I also think that it is appropriate to take advantage of "minilateral" opportunities, whereby smaller collection of states could meet for more intimate gatherings to discuss specific applications of the Guidelines.

In addition to multilateral strategic dialogue, there is also a very important "in-country" role for the Japanese. It is not for me to talk about the legislative challenge that lies ahead for Prime Minister Hashimoto's government. However, the fact of the matter is that for us to realize the full potential of the Guidelines, there will need to be some aggressive legislative changes in Japan.

Finally, the ultimate goal of the Guidelines is to allow our military planners and bureaucrats to engage with their Japanese counterparts on a host of regional security challenges. In this respect, we think that it is extremely important to allow those in Japan who are ultimately responsible for regional security to begin the process of closer consultation, simultaneously and at various levels, on a whole range of issues.